# GREAT OPERA SINGERS
# OF THE TWENTIETH CENTURY
## 1927-1990

# GREAT OPERA SINGERS
# OF THE TWENTIETH CENTURY
## 1927-1990

Donald S. Blair

The Edwin Mellen Press
Lewiston/Queenston/Lampeter

**Library of Congress Cataloging-in-Publication Data**

Blair, Donald S.
    Great opera singers of the twentieth century, 1927-1990 / Donald
S. Blair
        p.  cm.
    Includes bibliographical references and index.
    ISBN 0-7734-9850-8
    1. Singers--Biography.    I. Title.
ML400.B55    1991
782. 1'092'2--dc20                                        90-29109
[B]                                                          CIP
                                                             MN

A CIP catalog record for this book
is available from the British Library.

The Edwin Mellen Press              The Edwin Mellen Press
        Box 450                             Box 67
Lewiston, New York                  Queenston, Ontario
      USA  14092                      CANADA  L0S 1L0

The Edwin Mellen Press, Ltd.
Lampeter, Dyfed, Wales
UNITED KINGDOM  SA48 7DY

Printed in the United States of America

In loving memory of my parents,
Oscar and Bertha,
and my wife, Marguerite.

# TABLE OF CONTENTS

Introduction...................................................................................................iii

Foreword.......................................................................................................v

*Sopranos* ....................................................................................................1

    Licia Albanese...........................................................................3
    Montserrat Caballé....................................................................5
    Kirsten Flagstad ........................................................................7
    Dorothy Kirsten.......................................................................11
    Claudia Muzio .........................................................................13
    Birgit Nilsson ..........................................................................15
    Roberta Peters.........................................................................17
    Lily Pons.................................................................................19
    Leontyne Price........................................................................21
    Elizabeth Rethberg..................................................................23
    Beverly Sills............................................................................25
    Renata Scotto .........................................................................27
    Teresa Stratas.........................................................................29
    Joan Sutherland.......................................................................31
    Renata Tebaldi........................................................................33

*Tenors* ......................................................................................................35

    Jussi Bjoerling........................................................................36
    José Carreras ..........................................................................37
    Franco Corelli.........................................................................39
    Richard Crooks .......................................................................41
    Mario Del Monaco ..................................................................45
    Beniamino Gigli......................................................................47
    Jan Kiepura.............................................................................49
    Charles Kullman .....................................................................50
    Giovanni Martinelli.................................................................53
    John McCormack.....................................................................54
    Lauritz Melchior.....................................................................57
    Jan Peerce..............................................................................59
    Tito Schipa .............................................................................61
    Richard Tucker .......................................................................63

*Mezzo-Sopranos*........................................................................................67

    Marilyn Horne........................................................................69
    Regina Resnik ........................................................................71
    Ernestine Schumann-Heink .....................................................72
    Giulietta Simionato .................................................................73

Risë Stevens...................................................................................77
Ebe Stignani...................................................................................78
Gladys Swarthout.............................................................................79

*Baritones*......................................................................................81

Ettore Bastianini.............................................................................82
Igor Gorin ......................................................................................84
Cornell MacNeil..............................................................................87
Robert Merrill.................................................................................89
John Charles Thomas........................................................................91
Lawrence Tibbett.............................................................................95
Leonard Warren...............................................................................99
Robert Weede................................................................................101

*Basses*........................................................................................103

Salvatore Baccaloni........................................................................105
Jerome Hines.................................................................................107
Alexander Kipnis ...........................................................................108
Ezio Pinza ....................................................................................109
Paul Plishka..................................................................................113
Georgio Tozzi................................................................................115

Active – Present Day Sopranos, Tenors,
Mezzo-Sopranos, Baritones and Basses ......................................117

Other Singers, Past and Present,
Whom I Regard Highly .............................................................123

Bibliography................................................................................129

Index..........................................................................................133

Frank Guarrera as Valentin
in *Faust*

# INTRODUCTION

Donald S. Blair, throughout his adolescent and mature years, has perhaps heard more singers in a period of sixty three years than all but a very few people now living. He heard in person almost all of the truly great singers in that period of time, and he also acquired a vast collection of recordings (2,463) which go back to the time of Patti, Caruso, Farrar, Schumann-Heink, Scotti, and Journet. From that time Mr. Blair brings us up to the present-day singers, such as Pavarotti, Domingo, L. Price, Sutherland, Horne, Milnes, Ghiaurov, and many others.

Mr. Blair has "singled-out" for special consideration certain voices in the soprano, mezzo-soprano, tenor, baritone, and bass categories, all of whom he has personally heard in opera or concert, many of them a number of times. He has studied the art of other singers through early or late recordings, through radio and television, and through movies. In his assessment of quality of voice and performance, Mr. Blair often distinguishes between singing-actors, singing-actresses, and pure vocalists, in each voice category.

Frank Guarrera

# FOREWORD

Over a period of sixty-three years it has been my privilege to hear many great singers. The fifty I have chosen for discussion in this book were all heard by me in person, most of them several times, often in company with my family. All of the singers have enriched my life, and they have contributed to the sum total of joy in the world. I salute them in gratitude.

I am pleased and grateful too, that over the years I have had the privilege of corresponding with such great music critics as: Sir Rudolf Bing, Irving Kolodin, Henry Pleasants, Gaetano Merola, Carol Fox, Martin Mayer, Alexander Fried, Richard Mohr, T. A. McEwen, Speight Jenkins, Ray Minshull, and Robin May.

The above people are in no way responsible for any personal opinions I have expressed in this book. I am indebted to them, nevertheless, for adding to my love and appreciation of great music and great singers.

I would also like to express appreciation to Frank Guarrera, many years a leading baritone at the Metropolitan Opera Association and now a professor emeritus of music at the University of Washington, for writing the introduction to this book.

Mr. Guarrera, the famous American baritone, was born in Philadelphia in 1923 of Sicilian parents. He studied voice with the renowned baritone Richard Bonelli, and Mr. Guarrera also graduated from the Curtis Institute of Music.

In 1948 Frank Guarrera won the Metropolitan Opera Auditions of the Air contest. He made his debut in 1948 at the Metropolitan as Escamillo in *Carmen*. Arturo Toscanini helped Mr. Guarrera to appear at La Scala, and later (in 1953) Frank Guarrera was chosen by Toscanini to sing Ford in the conductor's N.B.C. radio production of *Falstaff*.

Mr. Guarrera also appeared in opera in London, Paris, San Francisco, Chicago, and Los Angeles, among other international centers. I heard him sing several times in San Francisco. He was much loved there. Altogether Mr. Guarrera had a very remarkable career in opera and in the concert and recording fields. His voice was one of great beauty and he was also an exceptionally fine actor.

Among his many great roles in opera, Frank Guarrera's Valentin in *Faust* was a classic. Will the beauty of his voice and power in "Avant de quitter ces lieux" ever be surpassed. As a superb singer and actor, he appeared in casts with other famous artists such as: Tucker, Pons, Corelli, Tebaldi, Siepi, Del Monaco, Kirsten, Conley, Steber, Hines, Baccaloni, Albanese, Corena, Sills, Valletti, Swarthout, Kullman, Simionato, and Rossi-Lemeni.

In addition to his having been a great singer, Frank Guarrera and his lovely wife, Adelina, are beautiful people.

Appreciation is also due my daughters, Kathleen and Barbara, for suggesting that I write this book and for their unfailing encouragement at every stage. Barbara and Carol Rodin assisted expertly in the preparation of the manuscript.

Through the courtesy and kindness of Mr. Robert Tuggle, Director of the Metropolitan Opera Archives, and Mr. John Pennino we have the beautiful pictures of the singers that appear in this book. I want to express much appreciation to them and to their staff for their help.

I would also like to thank Professor Herbert W. Richardson, my publisher, for his assistance in making this book possible.

Donald S. Blair

# SOPRANOS, TENORS, MEZZO-SOPRANOS, BARITONES AND BASSES

# SOPRANOS

# LICIA ALBANESE

Licia Albanese, soprano, was born on July 22, 1913, in Bari, Italy. She began her studies at the Bari Conservatory and then studied voice with Giuseppina Baldassare-Tedeschi. Miss Albanese made her debut in Bari in 1934 as Mimi in *La Bohème*. After 1935 she was a much admired singer at the Arena Festival and La Scala opened its arms to her. Beniamino Gigli was delighted to be her partner at La Scala. After singing in many places in Italy, she joined the Metropolitan Opera in 1940, making her debut as Butterfly in the opera *Madame Butterfly*.

Miss Albanese's greatest triumph at the Met was in 1942 as Violetta in *La Traviata*. She sang at the Metropolitan Opera for twenty years and was acclaimed all over Europe and America in her guest appearances.

I heard Miss Albanese the evening of September 13, 1946, at the Civic Auditorium in Seattle. She was appearing with The San Francisco Opera Company in Verdi's *La Traviata*. She was the Violetta to Jan Peerce's Alfredo. Several others in the cast were: Valentino, Cehanovsky, and Votipka. The conductor was the famous Gaetano Merola.

She greeted Mrs. Blair and me very warmly when we went backstage after the opera to visit with her. When we were about to leave, she said. "Don't you want my autograph?" Indeed we did, and to this day we prize it and keep it along with the autographs of Gigli, Peerce, Kullman, Tibbett, J. C. Thomas, Kirsten, Warren, Pons, Tebaldi, Baccaloni, Pinza, and others of the great singers.

Miss Albanese stands high in my estimate of the great singers.

Montserrat Caballé

# MONTSERRAT CABALLÉ

Montserrat Caballé, lyric soprano, was born on April 12, 1933, in Barcelona. She was from a musical family and studied voice at the Conservatory in Barcelona. She sang at the Municipal Theater in Basel from 1957-1960. Then Bremen called her for the years 1960-1962. In 1962-63, she sang in a number of cities and made a concert tour of Mexico. In 1963 she made her Barcelona debut. On April 20, 1965, she substituted for Marilyn Horne in New York in a concert performance of *Lucrezia Borgia* and had an overwhelming success. In 1966 she was signed to a Metropolitan Opera contract and has remained a member of that venerable company ever since. The next year (1967) she was given an unusually great opportunity for a singer so new to the Met. She was awarded the role of Violetta in *La Traviata* in the first performance of the season. She sang to great acclaim.

Miss Caballé has now sung all over the world. She has appeared in Argentina, Austria, Brazil, Vancouver (Canada), France, Germany, Hungary, Italy (La Scala), Mexico City, Portugal, Spain, Switzerland, London (Covent Garden), Russia, and with all of the major opera companies in the United States. I know of no more widely traveled opera singer.

Miss Caballé sings the leading roles from the operas of the following composers, among others: Bellini, Boito, Cilea, Donizetti, Giordano, Gounod, Leoncavallo, Massenet, Mozart, Puccini, Rossini, Strauss, Verdi and Wagner. It is almost unbelievable how many operas from the works of each composer in which Miss Caballé has performed.

In my opinion Miss Caballé is the greatest lyric-dramatic soprano in the world today. That is not at all to minimize the greatness of such stars as Scotto, Freni, Stratas, Cotrubas, Kiri te Kanawa, Riciarelli, and others. But for me the voice of Caballé has a number of great qualities that do not exist to the same extent in any other lyric-soprano presently singing.

I last heard Miss Caballé in concert at the Seattle Opera House in September, 1981. Her rendition of "Vissi d'arte" from *Tosca*, and her other Puccini and Verdi arias caused an ecstatic ovation such I have seldom heard in any opera house.

Mr. Martin Bernheimer of the Los Angeles Times wrote not long ago, "Caballé molded phrases with introspective finesse, capitalizing on a gorgeous legato and a floating pianissimo, finally opening all the stops for fearless, radiant, thrilling assaults on the high climaxes. This was a vocal tour de force."

I agree with Mr. Bernheimer's assessment of the vocal prowess of Miss Caballé. But as an actress in opera, she cannot equal her vocal achievement.

My generalization is that Miss Caballé as a vocalist among lyric-dramatic sopranos has no peer today. But there are others in her voice classification who are greater singing-actresses. Some of these would be Scotto, Freni, Stratas, Kiri te Kanawa, Ricciarelli, Cotrubas, Dimitrova, and Vaness.

# KIRSTEN FLAGSTAD

Kirsten Flagstad, soprano, was born on July 12, 1895, in Hamar, Norway, and died on December 8, 1962, in Oslo. She studied voice with Ellen Schytte-Jacobsen in Oslo and made her opera debut there in 1913 as Nuri in *Tiefland*. She studied further with Albert Westwang in Oslo and Gillis Bratt in Stockholm. She returned to Oslo in 1917 to do minor roles at the Mayol Theatre, and she also specialized in operettas. She then, in 1921 made a tour of France. After that, she was engaged at the City Theatre in Gothenburg, Sweden from 1928-32.

In 1933 Miss Flagstad appeared at the Bayreuth Festival and in 1934 had her first great success there as Sieglinde in *Die Walküre* and as Gutrune in *Götterdämmerung*. Because of her continuing success she was engaged by the Metropolitan Opera in 1935 as Sieglinde. Almost overnight she became one of the most outstanding Wagner sopranos of her time because of her great performance as Sieglinde. At the Metropolitan Opera she went from one triumph to another until 1941, when she left because of World War II.

Miss Flagstad also had great successes at Covent Garden, the Vienna State Opera, and in San Francisco, Chicago, and Zurich. Because of the war she lived in retirement in her native Norway between 1941-45. She made a tour of the United States in 1947-48 and sang often at Covent Garden between 1948-51. She was also greatly admired as Leonora in *Fidelio* at the Salzburg Festivals in the opera year of 1949-50.

In 1951 Miss Flagstad returned to London and appeared at the Mermaid Theater in *Dido and Aeneas*. Then in 1952, for her performance in *Alceste*, the Metropolitan Opera audience gave her a great ovation. She made her farewell stage appearances in 1955. She then became director of the opera houses in Oslo (from 1958-60)

I heard Miss Flagstad with Lauritz Melchior and Alexander Kipnis in the War Memorial Opera House in San Francisco in *Tristan and Isolde* during the 1939 opera season. I shall always be grateful for having had the privilege of hearing Kirsten Flagstad, who many critics believe was the

Kirsten Flagstad
in *Tristan and Isolde*

greatest dramatic soprano of all time. Very often she was called the "Caruso in Petticoats." Her voice was big, extremely beautiful with a dark quality. The voice also had great artistic expressiveness, and she had an unfailingly accurate technique. She was an absolute "wonder."

Dorothy Kirsten as Minnie in
*La Fanciulla del West*

# DOROTHY KIRSTEN

Dorothy Kirsten, lyric soprano, was born in 1917 in Montclair, New Jersey. One of her first jobs was that of a telephone operator. She then studied singing with Louis Dornay and Betsy Dornay-Culp in New York. Grace Moore, the splendid opera star, first noticed Dorothy Kirsten in 1938 and then assisted her with her career. After further study with Astolfo Pescia in Italy, Miss Kirsten sang in a concert at the New York World's Fair in 1940. She made her opera debut in the same year in *Manon* at the Chicago Opera.

In 1942 Miss Kirsten sang with the San Carlo Opera Company and made a highly successful appearance in New York in the *Merry Widow*. After she had appeared at the New York City Opera, in San Francisco, and in Montreal, she joined the Metropolitan Opera Company in 1945 as Mimi in *La Bohème*. Since then, she has been a long-time revered member on the Met roster and has made guest appearances in South America, particularly at the Teatro Colón. She also sang in England in 1952 and made a tour of Russia in 1962.

She is a beautiful woman with a beautiful voice. I heard her with the San Francisco Opera Company in 1946, when the company came to Seattle. She appeared as Mimi in *La Bohéme*, and her partner, for that evening, Rodolfo, was Charles Kullman. They both sang magnificently to a packed house.

In 1969 Dorothy Kirsten sang the title role of Floria, in *Tosca*, with the Seattle Opera Company. She sang "Vissi d' arte, vissi d' amore" as expertly as I have ever heard it sung. When Mrs. Blair and I went backstage to see if we could greet Miss Kirsten, she was, to quote Mrs. Blair, "absolutely adorable, both in looks and graciousness." She gave her best all through her performance, and her best certainly thrilled the great audience who came to see and hear her.

Some of the outstanding sopranos of the Kirsten era were: Albanese, Moffo, Costa, Tucci, De Los Angeles, Rysanek, Rothenberger, Della

Casa, Amara, Callas, Farrell, Munsel, Harshaw, Steber, Curtis-Verna, Schwarzkopf, and Arroyo.

Also a singer of this era who made her mark primarily in motion pictures, concerts, and on recordings, was the lovely Jeanette MacDonald.

# CLAUDIA MUZIO

I heard Miss Muzio with the Chicago Civic Opera Comnpany (now Chicago Lyric) in *La Traviata*, with Tito Schipa and John Charles Thomas in the other major roles, in March of 1931 in Seattle.

Miss Muzio was born February 7, 1889, in Pavia, Italy, and died May 24, 1936, in Rome. In 1911 she made her debut as the heroine in *Manon Lescaut* in Arezzo, Italy. After several successes in minor opera houses in Italy, she was greatly admired in the 1913-14 season at La Scala as Desdemona in *Otello* and as Fiora in *L'Amore dei Tre Re*. She sang at Covent Garden in 1914, and in 1916 she was engaged by the Metropolitan Opera, making her debut brilliantly in *Tosca*. She remained as a bright light at the Met until 1921, when she left to sing at the Chicago Opera (1922-32). Then, before returning to the Met in 1934, she sang in opera houses in South America and Cuba. Two of her greatest roles, among many in Chicago and at the Met, were Violetta in *La Traviata*, and Santuzza in *Cavalleria Rusticana*.

In the Violetta role, because of her gorgeous voice and her great acting, I place her among the greatest singing actresses I ever heard. Because of her eminence in the art of acting, she was called "The Duse of Opera." It was a great loss to the music world when she died so young.

Birgit Nilsson as Turandot

# BIRGIT NILSSON

Birgit Nilsson, dramatic soprano, was born on May 17, 1918, near Karup, Sweden. She studied at the Royal Conservatory in Stockholm from 1941-46 and made her debut there at the Royal Opera in 1944. The first role of significance she sang there was Agathe in *Der Freischütz*.

In 1948 she made a successful tour of Germany and Italy. In 1951 she was applauded greatly for her singing of Elektra in *Idomeneo* at the Glyndebourne Festival. At this point in her career her voice gradually changed from a lyric to a dramatic soprano. Many critics believe that she became the most famous Wagner soprano of her time.

Miss Nilsson went from one triumph to another at La Scala, Covent Garden, the State operas in Vienna and Munich, and at the Dusseldorf Opera. In 1954 she sang Elsa in *Lohengrin* at the Bayreuth Festival. Since then she has created a great stir in her annual appearances there, especially as Brunnhilde in the Ring Cycle and as Isolde in *Tristan and Isolde*.

Miss Nilsson on coming to the United States became very famous, especially as Turandot. Beginning in 1956 she had great successes in San Francisco, Los Angeles, and Chicago. She made her debut at the Metropolitan Opera in 1959 as Isolde.

I heard Miss Nilsson at the Seattle Opera House, as Turandot, in 1969. Regine Crespin, as Liu, was in the same cast. Elsewhere, in Turandot, the team of Nilsson, Corelli, and Scotto made great news.

Miss Nilsson became world famous. She had a big, beautiful voice, clarity of tone, and brilliant stage presence. Although she was primarily a Wagner singer, she did appear in some Verdi and Puccini roles. Because of her earned world renown, it would not be out of place to compare Miss Nilsson very favorably with Flagstad, Traubel, Ponselle, Rethberg, Jeritza, Milanov, Albanese, Tebaldi, Callas and L. Price.

Roberta Peters as Zerlina
in Mozart's *Don Giovanni*

# ROBERTA PETERS

Roberta Peters, coloratura soprano, was born May 4, 1930, in New York. Originally, her family came from Austria. She took vocal lessons with William Hermann in New York City. In 1950 she made her operatic debut at the Metropolitan, when she replaced an ailing colleague in the role of Zerlina in *Don Giovanni*. She was so well received that in 1951 she became a member of the Met. She has remained there, with great distinction, ever since. She was particularly admired at the Metropolitan as the Queen of the Night in *Die Zauberflöte* and in Italian Opera. She has had great success in guest appearances in Seattle, San Francisco, and Chicago, and in concert appearances all over the U.S.A. In 1951 she sang at Covent Garden and in 1957 on a number of Italian stages. She has made successful concert tours in Russia, and she was greatly admired as Queen of the Night at the Salzburg festivals in 1963-64. She has a brilliant coloratura voice which she used with much intelligence and with great virtuosity.

Some of Miss Peters greatest successes have been in the operas *Il Barbiere di siviglia, Un Ballo in Maschera, Rigoletto, Orphée et Eurydice, Lucia di Lammermoor*, and *Ariadne auf Naxos*.

I heard Miss Peters, in concert at Seattle's Orpheum Theatre, the evening of June 2, 1955. She was assisted at the piano by Warner Bass and flutist Samuel Pratt.

She was and is a beautiful woman. She changed gowns during the intermission, and both were absolutely gorgeous. The way she curtsied and bowed after applause impressed both Mrs. Blair and me. Neither of us had seen such grace and charm in a curtsy before.

As to her voice, it was a pure, beautiful, flexible instrument, with adequate power. The way she and her flutist followed each other up and down the scale in such songs as "Lo! Hear the Gentle Lark" was unbelievably thrilling. Other songs and arias that produced great audience acclaim were: "Clair de lune" (Debussy), "Caro Nome" from *Rigoletto*, "Swiss Echo Song", "Last Rose of Summer", and "Sempra Libra" from *La Traviata*.

Hearing Roberta Peters that evening was one of the most enjoyable occasions in my lifetime. She came to Seattle again in 1964-65 to the Opera House as Lucia in *Lucia di Lammermoor*. "Her Mad Scene" produced an ovation seldom equalled in this city or elsewhere.

As a coloratura soprano, Miss Peters brought back memories of Galli-Curci and Pons.

# LILY PONS

Lily Pons, coloratura soprano, was born on April 13, 1904, near Cannes, France. She studied piano starting at the age of 13. This musical training took place at the Paris National Conservatory. She studied voice in Paris with Albert di Gorostiaga and made her stage debut in 1928, in Mulhouse, singing the title role in *Lakmé*.

Miss Pons then sang in French provincial opera houses. She was heard by Giovanni Zenatello, the great tenor, who was instrumental in getting her into the Metropolitan in 1931. Her debut there in *Lucia di Lammermoor* was nothing short of a sensation, as was her appearance in 1932 as *Lakmé*. For 30 years Miss Pons was one of the brightest of lights at the Metropolitan.

She sang at Covent Garden, the two great Paris Opera Houses, the Teatro Colón, and in Brussels, Chicago, and San Francisco. Her concert tours took her through Europe, North and South America, and to Mexico and Cuba. She also had a very successful film career in Hollywood.

Although Miss Pons' coloratura soprano voice was not a big one, it was ample in size, on the order of Tetrazzini's and Galli-Curci's. Miss Pons, without question, was one of the greatest coloratura sopranos in the long history of the Metropolitan. Her voice was both beautiful and effortless.

I heard Miss Pons in person in San Francisco in 1940, at the World's Fair. She was accompanied by her husband, André Kostelanetz and his orchestra. Miss Pons sang to an overflow crowd, who greeted her very enthusiastically. Her program included such arias as the Mad Scene from *Lucia*, Verdi's "Caro Nome", the "Bell Song" from *Lakmé*, and "Una Voce Poco Fa", from the *Barber of Seville*.

Miss Pons was a great artist in every way.

Leontyne Price as Aïda

# LEONTYNE PRICE

Leontyne Price, lirico spinto soprano, was born in 1929 in Laurel, Miss. and studied voice at the Julliard School of Music. She also took voice training with Florence Page Kimball in New York.

In 1951 Miss Price made a tour of Europe in *Porgy and Bess*. As Bess, she was partnered with great success in London, Paris, Berlin, and Moscow, with the baritone, William Warfield. In 1954, Miss Price had a great success in a concert at Town Hall in New York. This was followed immediately by her being warmly received as Aïda in the opera companies of Chicago and San Francisco.

In 1957 Miss Price toured Italy as a concert singer and made highly successful appearances that year at La Scala in the opera *Aïda*. In 1958 she triumphed in the same role at the Arena Festival. Miss Price has appeared very often as a guest artist at the opera houses in Vienna, London, Paris, and Berlin. In 1960 she was celebrated for her portrayal of Donna Anna in *Don Giovanni* at the Salzburg Festival. The same year she made her Metropolitan Opera debut as Leonora in *Il Trovatore*, with Franco Corelli as Manrico. Miss Price has sung regularly at the Met ever since. In 1966 she created the role of Cleopatra in *Anthony and Cleopatra*, which had its world premier as the opening production at the Metropolitan Opera's new home in Lincoln Center.

I heard Miss Price in 1961, 1963, and 1965 at the War Memorial Opera House in San Francisco. The operas were *Madame Butterfly, Aïda*, and *La Forza Del Destino*. Some of her partners were Kónya, Resnik, and Tozzi. The conductors were Adler (in *Butterfly*) and Molinari-Pradelli (in *Aïda* and *La Forza Del Destino*).

Miss Price has an opulent beautiful soprano voice – one of the greatest in our time. In my opinion it compares very favorably with Ponselle, Rethberg, Albanese, Milanov, Nilsson, Callas, and Tebaldi.

# ELIZABETH RETHBERG

Elizabeth Rethberg, soprano, was born on September 22, 1894, in Schwarzenberg, Germany. In 1912-13 she studied, first piano and then singing, at the Dresden Conservatory, and finally singing with Otto Watrin. She made her opera debut in 1915 at Dresden as Agathe in *Der Freischütz*. She remained a principal singer at Dresden until 1922, when she was offered a contract at the Metropolitan Opera. There she had monumental triumphs from 1922-42.

Guest appearances brought her one success after another when she appeared in Havana in 1923 and 1928, Covent Garden in 1925, La Scala and the Rome Opera in 1929. She was then heard all over her native Germany and at the Salzburg Festivals. She married the Met baritone George Cehanovsky in 1957.

I heard Miss Rethburg at the San Francisco Opera in its 1938-39 season. The opera was *Don Giovanni*. With her was a remarkable cast of Pinza, Jessner, Favero, Baccaloni, and Borgioli. The conductor was Fritz Reiner.

Miss Rethberg's voice was one of exquisite tonal beauty. She had complete mastery in the technique of singing, and she was an excellent actress. Arturo Toscanini once remarked, "Elizabeth Rethberg has the most beautiful soprano voice I have ever heard."

Because of Miss Rethberg's world-wide renown and my love for her voice, I would rate her equal to such great stars as Ponselle, Farrar, Jeritza, Milanov, Tebaldi, Callas, and Leontyne Price.

Beverly Sills as Violetta in
*La Traviata*

# BEVERLY SILLS

Beverly Sills, coloratura soprano, was born on May 26, 1929, in New York.  She studied voice with Estelle Liebling there.  Her debut as Micaela in *Carmen* was with the Philadelphia Opera in 1948.  Several universities, including Harvard, have granted her honorary doctorates in Music.

Miss Sills has sung at such places as the New York City Opera, the Metropolitan, and many other United States opera companies.  She has had great acceptance in foreign countries also.  These include the Vienna Staatsoper, Buenos Aires, Berlin Deutsche Opera, La Scala (Milan), Naples, Venice, Mexico City, Geneva, London Royal Opera, and many more.

I heard Miss Sills as Lucia in the Seattle Opera production of *Lucia di Lammermoor* in the 1971-72 season.  She was absolutely fabulous.  Her tones were clear, flexible, beautiful, and of ample size.  Her rendition of the "Mad Scene" was so powerful as to create almost chaos in the packed opera house.  I had heard her previously in *La Bohème* and *Tales of Hoffman*, to great acclaim from the audiences and newspapers.

Miss Sills is a great personality even apart from her gorgeous singing.  She appears on talk shows and is the mistress of ceremonies for many nationally televised broadcasts of musical programs as well as other programs of note.  She has a friendly, winsome disposition and is generally an extrovert in the best sense of the term.  She was until recently General Manager of the New York City Opera Company.

As a singer in her prime, there is no question but that she was one of the world's great coloratura sopranos.  Joan Sutherland's voice was and is larger, and perhaps Galli-Curci's, Pons', and Peters' voices had a little more "sheen" and beauty in them.  But taking attributes as a whole, Miss Sills is certainly in the same class of coloratura sopranos as Tetrazzini, Galli-Curci, Pons, Sayão, Sutherland and Peters.

Renata Scotto as Lucia
in *Lucia di Lammermoor*

# RENATA SCOTTO

Renata Scotto, lyric soprano, was born on February 24, 1935, in Savona, Italy. She made her opera debut at La Scala in 1954 as Walter in *La Wally*. All of the largest Italian opera houses sought out her services, with La Scala and the Rome Opera especially bidding for her.

Because of Miss Scotto's Italian successes, she appeared in guest appearances all over the world. She sang frequently at Covent Garden, where she appeared as Amina in *La Sonnambula* in 1958. She triumphed also in other coloratura roles from Italian opera at the Vienna State Opera and in Chicago and San Francisco. She made her debut at the Metropolitan Opera during the 1965-66 season as Madame Butterfly and has appeared there often since that time.

I heard Miss Scotto, in December of 1981, at the Metropolitan Opera in New York as Musetta in *La Bohème*. She had done Mimi before, but this particular time she wanted to do the role of Musetta. Other members of the cast were Stratas, Carreras, and Morris.

Miss Scotto was beautifully dressed in a red gown and the audience dearly loved her rendition of "Musetta's Waltz." Her entire performance seemed to be almost perfect. She is certainly among the top four or five singing-actresses in the world today–perhaps even higher than that in rank. She partnered with Ettore Bastianini, the great baritone, in recordings of *Lucia, Rigoletto*, and *La Traviata* that hardly can be improved upon for beauty and vocal fervor.

Miss Scotto first rocked the music world when she substituted for Maria Callas in a performance of *La Sonnambula* in 1957 at the Edinburgh Festival.

Teresa Stratas as Nedda
in *I Pagliacci*

# TERESA STRATAS

Teresa Stratas, lyric soprano, was born in 1938 in Toronto, Canada. She studied voice at the conservatory in Toronto and made her debut there in 1958.

In 1959 Miss Stratas won the Metropolitan Opera auditions in New York and has been engaged at the Metropolitan since 1960. She has had great acclaim at the Met and has become one of the principal prima donnas there.

Miss Stratas has triumphed in Moscow, London, Germany, and many other places in the world. She has been especially appreciated at other U.S.A. opera houses as well as at the Metropolitan Opera. Miss Stratas received accolades for her Cio-Cio-San in San Francisco in 1966.

While I was in New York City in December of 1981, I heard Miss Stratas as Mimi at the Metropolitan Opera. Among members of the cast with her in *La Bohème* were José Carreras as Rodolfo and Renata Scotto as Musetta.

Miss Stratas presented us with a tragic Mimi. She had a big, beautiful, technically trained voice, and in all respects was a believable Mimi. Her rendition of "Si mi chimano Mimi" almost took down the House. Her duets with Carreras were also sensational.

I have heard many Mimis, but never a better one than Teresa Stratas'. With all due recognition of her great acclaim around the world, I still feel strongly that she has not yet received the appreciation that she merits.

Joan Sutherland as Marie
in *La Fille Du Régiment*

# JOAN SUTHERLAND

Joan Sutherland, dramatic coloratura soprano, was born on November 7, 1926, in Sydney, Australia. She studied singing with John and Aida Dickens in Sydney and sang the title role in *Judith* there in 1950. She went to London in 1951 to study with Clive Carey. She made her debut at Covent Garden in 1952 as the First Lady in *Die Zauberflte*. At first she sang heavier roles: as Amelia in *Un Ballo in Maschera*, Agathe in *Der Freischtz*, and Eva in *Die Meistersinger*.

In 1958-59 she changed her roles to those of a coloratura soprano and appeared at Covent Garden as Lucia in *Lucia di Lammermoor*, Amina in *La Sonnambula*, and Violetta in *La Traviata* – to great applause. Miss Sutherland made guest appearances in Vienna in 1959 and in Genoa, Parma, and Venice in 1960. In 1961 she was rapturously received at La Scala in *Beatrice di Tenda*. She has also sung with overwhelming success at the Paris Opera, at the Glyndebourne and Edinburgh Festivals, and in Cologne, Barcelona, San Francisco, and Seattle.

The Metropolitan Opera in 1961 engaged Miss Sutherland to make her debut there in *Lucia*. She was given thunderous applause on that occasion and has sung at the Met many times since. She is married to the conductor Richard Bonynge.

Miss Sutherland came to Seattle in the 1970-71 opera season. I heard her in *The Tales of Hoffmann*. She sang all three of the major soprano roles – those of Olympia, Giulietta, and Antonia. The audience went almost completely berserk over her performance. The newspapers likened this appearance to her great triumph in Seattle in the 1966-67 season in the opera *Lakm*, when, after she had sung the "Bell Song", the audience would hardly let her leave the stage so that the rest of the opera could continue.

There is no doubt that Miss Sutherland must be considered one of the greatest, if not the greatest, coloratura soprano of this century. Other coloraturas with whom she must be compared are: Tetrazzini, Galli-Curci, Pons, Sayo, and the great Americans – Peters and Sills. While Miss Sutherland's voice is heavier and she has more power than those ladies just mentioned, I sincerely believe that her voice is as beautiful and flexible as theirs for the coloratura roles.

Renata Tebaldi as Mimi
in *La Bohème*

# RENATA TEBALDI

Renata Tebaldi, lyric and dramatic soprano, was born February 1, 1922, in Pesaro, Italy. She made her debut in 1943 in Rovigo, Italy, as Elena in *Mefistofele*.

After World War II, through the good offices of Arturo Toscanini, she sang at La Scala, where since that time she has often been greatly admired. After 1950 she appeared at Covent Garden, at the Vienna State Opera, and in Paris, Rome, Naples, and Barcelona. She was paid great homage by the public everywhere.

In 1951 she made a guest appearance in San Francisco before going to the Met in 1955, where she received nothing but adulation for the beauty of her voice. She has literally performed all over the world in such places as Chicago, South America, Spain, Portugal, Holland, Germany, and France.

Renata Tebaldi is a beautiful woman and possessed of one of the greatest soprano voices of her time. Critics have applauded her for her clean intonation of her tones and for the elegance of her portrayals.

I heard her in 1965, in San Francisco, with Tucker and Bastianini in *Andrea Chénier* and have adored her voice ever since. She is at her very best in Puccini and Verdi roles.

Miss Tebaldi and Maria Callas were very often compared, as they were contemporaries in the opera world. They were very different in physical size, personality, and temperament. But the one thing that they had in common was that they were both great singers. In voice, Miss Callas could sing coloratura roles as well as dramatic roles – a great achievement – while Miss Tebaldi was solely a lyric-dramatic soprano. Also, Miss Callas was the greater actress. But at times she produced some strident top tones, while Miss Tebaldi did not. Although I acknowledge that Miss Callas was one of the greatest singing actresses of the century I must say that I always got more of a thrill from the vocal performance of Ponselle, Muzio, Rethberg, L. Price, Milanov, Tebaldi, and Caballé, than I did from that of Miss Callas.

Both Miss Tebaldi and Miss Callas disclaimed any animosity toward the other; but there is no question that the rivalry was intense, with each singer having a great many affectionados.

Both ladies stood in the very first rank of singers the world over.

# TENORS

# JUSSI BJOERLING

Jussi Bjoerling, tenor, was born February 2, 1911, in Stora Tuna, Sweden, and died on September 8, 1960 at his country home near Stockholm after a heart attack. Early in his life he toured the world in a vocal quartet with his father and two brothers.

In 1929 Bjoerling studied singing at the Royal Academy of Music in Stockholm as a pupil of John Forsell and in 1932 made his debut at the Royal Opera House there as Don Ottavio in *Don Giovanni*. His first successes came through appearances in Copenhagen, Prague, Vienna, and Budapest. He then had sensational triumphs at Covent Garden in London, followed by a concert in Carnegie Hall and a number of guest appearances at the Chicago Opera and in San Francisco.

In 1938 he made his debut at the Metropolitan as Rodolfo in *La Bohème*. Following the great acclaim from that debut, many countries made offers to him for concerts and opera appearances. From 1938-41, and then after World War II (from 1946 until his death in 1960), he was engaged at the Metropolitan Opera. In addition to his work in opera he was adjudged to be one of the great lights in concert and lieder singing.

It was as a concert singer that I heard him in Seattle at the Moore Theater. His voice was a God-given natural phenomenon with a shine on it, and he added to that a faultless technique, superb evenness of tone, and amazing breath control–coupled with supreme beauty of voice. The combination tells us why Jussi Bjoerling was adored by millions and proclaimed as having one of the most glorious voices of this century.

I shall never forget how this man, short in physical stature, "poured-out" his soul and voice in thrilling tones in "Cielo e mar" from *La Gioconda*, "Salut! demeure chaste" from *Faust*, "Questa o quella" from *Rigoletto*, "Di Quella Pira" from *Il Trovatore*, and "E lucevan le stelle" from *Tosca*. It was an evening I shall never forget.

Considering all of Mr. Bjoerling's great triumphs, I think it would be safe to say that from approximately 1945-1955 he had the most beautiful tenor voice in the world.

# JOSÉ CARRERAS

José Carreras, lyric tenor, was born in Spain and made his vocal debut in opera as Gennaro in *Lucrezia Borgia*, at the Teatro del Liceo, in Barcelona, in 1970. He was a chemistry student but gave up all serious thoughts of being a chemist when he realized what a God-given voice he had.

Mr. Carreras sings with all the major opera companies in Argentina, Austria, Belgium, Czechoslovakia, France, Germany, Hungary, Italy (La Scala), Spain, Switzerland, and England (London Royal Opera). In the United States he has sung in the opera houses of such cities as Chicago, Dallas, New York (Met), Philadelphia, San Francisco, and in concert at the Seattle Opera House.

I heard José Carreras at the Metropolitan Opera House in New York during the 1981 season. The opera was *La Bohème*. Others in the cast were Teresa Stratas, Renata Scotto, and James Morris.

Mr. Carreras is a handsome man, not large in size, but possesses a lyric tenor voice with great range and volume, enough to fill adequately the great Metropolitan Opera House. He was an outstanding Rodolfo. The audience showed great enthusiasm for him, especially when he sang "Che Gelinda Manina" and in the beautiful duets with Teresa Stratas. He is a fine actor also.

Mrs. Blair, my daughters, Kathleen and Barbara, and their husbands and I later heard Mr. Carreras in concert at the Seattle Opera House. He was in great voice and gave us a very memorable concert. He is at his absolute best when he is singing in the operas of Verdi, Puccini, Bellini, and Donizetti.

I believe that Mr. Carreras will continue to have a splendid career. I feel that he is about number three in the world today, behind Pavarotti and Domingo. Since he is younger than either of those gentlemen, it is conceivable that at some point in time he could become the number one tenor in the world.

Franco Corelli as Radames
in *Aïda*

# FRANCO CORELLI

Franco Corelli, tenor, was born in 1925 in Ancona, Italy. He turned down a civil service career after vocal studies at the Conservatories of Pesaro and Milan. In 1950 he won a singing contest in Florence, and in 1952 he made his opera debut. For three years he sang on provincial stages and on the radio in Italy. Then in 1954 he sang at La Scala. He quickly attained stardom on all the more important stages in Italy and at the Maggio Musicale and Arena Festivals.

Mr. Corelli made guest appearances at the Vienna State Opera, Covent Garden, the Paris Opera, and the San Francisco, Seattle and Chicago Operas. In 1960 he had a very successful debut at the Metropolitan Opera in *Il Trovatore* – he as Manrico and Leontyne Price as Leonora. Mr. Corelli sang the same role at the Salzburg Festival in 1962.

Mrs. Blair, our daughters and their husbands and I first heard Franco Corelli in opera at the Seattle Opera House during the 1967-68 season. The opera was *Romeo and Juliet*: Franco Corelli as Romeo; and Gianna D'Angelo, as the pretty and beautiful-voiced, Juliet.

Mr. Corelli could be the most ideal Romeo ever. His streamlined, 6-foot-plus frame, and handsome face has never been exceeded in Hollywood, to my knowledge. His fresh and radiant tenor voice, of great power and brilliance in timbre, took the opera house by storm. I shall never forget his rendition of "O nuit! Sous tes ailes obscures...Ah! leve-toi, soleil!" At the end of the aria he went from a fortissimo to as beautiful a pianissimo as I have ever heard.

My honest belief is that between 1965 and 1975 Franco Corelli was the greatest tenor on earth. Mr. Tucker, who had been the supreme tenor just earlier, was slowing down a little vocally, I think, when Corelli was at his absolute peak. But Mr. Corelli was ten years younger than Mr. Tucker.

Alan Rich, of the New York Herald Tribune wrote, "It is Mr. Corelli, hands down. There is no tenor in modern times, Italian or otherwise, whose voice rings out with greater vibrancy, whose every tone carries with it emotion at white heat. The sounds he makes, seemingly without effort, are dazzlingly bright, urgent and communicative."

Sir Rudolf Bing, in his book "A Knight at the Opera," said of Franco Corelli, "Hardly anybody doubted his world career and success. And indeed, he had it. In my view he is the greatest tenor of his day. He is also a warm-hearted human being."

Other great tenors who were at the Met at the time Corelli and Tucker, were there are Del Monaco, Di Stefano, Gedda, Bergonzi, Vickers, McCracken, Kraus, and King.

During the latter part of the Corelli career, Pavarotti and Domingo "came on" strongly. They are now receiving great world-wide acclaim, which they have so justly earned. In 1989, I heard Mr. Domingo in Seattle, and Mr. Pavarotti in Portland, Oregon. I believe that Mr. Pavarotti is the greatest tenor vocalist in the world today.

# RICHARD CROOKS

Richard Crooks, lyric tenor, was born on June 26, 1900, in Trenton, New Jersey. He caused much comment as a boy soprano in a church choir. After serving during World War I in the American Air Corps, he studied voice with Frank La Forge in New York and then became a soloist in a Presbyterian Church there. It was at this same church that Lawrence Tibbett sang when he was on his way to greatness.

Mr. Crooks had his first big success in 1923 when he gave nine concerts with the New York Symphony Orchestra under the director Walter Damrosch. In 1926 he started on a long concert tour in Europe. His opera debut occurred in 1927. On that occasion he sang Cavaradossi in *Tosca* at the Hamburg State Opera. This great success was followed by guest appearances in Berlin, Holland, Belgium, England, and Sweden. His first opera experience in the United States came with the Philadelphia Opera. The Metropolitan Opera called him in 1933 to perform as Des Grieux in *Manon*. His success there was instant, and he sang with the Metropolitan Opera until 1946.

Mr. Crooks was also a fine concert singer. His tours took him all over the world, including Africa and Australia. In 1946 he gave up his opera career.

I heard Mr. Crooks many times on National Radio Broadcasts, especially during the 1930s and 1940s. He sang on all the important radio broadcasts, such as "R.C.A.," "Magic Key," "Ford Sunday Evening Hour," and the "Bell Telephone Hour."

Mrs. Blair and I heard him twice in concert in Seattle when he was at the crest of his popularity. In both concerts he mixed operatic arias with Irish ballads. The response to his singing was standing ovations and thunderous applause.

Mr. Crooks was a lyric tenor and in the two concerts that we heard he sang: "Salut! demeure" from *Faust*, "Ah! leve-toi soleil!" from *Romeo et Juliette*, "Le Reve" from *Manon*, "Pourquoi me reveiller" from *Werther*, "Il mio tesoro" from *Don Giovanni*, "Una furtiva lagrima" from *L'Elisir d' Amore*, "E

Richard Crooks as Des Grieux
in *Manon*

lucevan le stelle" from *Tosca*, "Preslied" from *Die Meistersinger*, and "Amor ti vieta" from *Fedora*.

When it came to the Irish songs and other non-opera arias in the two concerts, he gave us the following numbers: "I Will Take You Home Again Kathleen," "Mother Machree," "Macushla," "Moonbeams" from the *Red Mill*, "The Green Hills of Ireland," "Songs My Mother Taught Me," "Only My Song," and the "Serenade" from the *Student Prince*. Very often some of his encore numbers were the same as John McCormack's.

Mr. Crooks had a gorgeous and beautifully trained voice. It was virile and had a sense of urgency in it. The three greatest lyric tenors I ever heard were Mc Cormack, Schipa, and Crooks.

I shall prize always the note I received from Mr. Crooks, when, in answer to my letter, he penned a "thank you" just shortly before he died in 1971.

Mario Del Monaco
in *Andrea Chénier*

# MARIO DEL MONACO

Mario Del Monaco, tenor, was born May 27, 1915 in Florence, Italy. He spent his youth in Pesaro and entered the conservatory there where he devoted himself to painting and sculpture. In Rome, at the age of 20, he won a prize in a singing contest arranged by Tullio Serafin, the conductor. During World War II Mr. Del Monaco was allowed a "leave" (in 1941) to make his debut at the Teatro Puccini. During the war he was able to appear only on rare occasions, but after the war's end his career developed very rapidly.

In 1946 Del Monaco created a sensation as Radames in *Aïda* at the Arena Festival, and in the same year he sang the title role in *Andrea Chënier* at Trieste. A highly successful tour in 1948 with the ensemble of the Teatro San Carlo made him internationally known. He then sang at La Scala, in London, Paris, and Vienna. In the summer of 1950 he was applauded at The Teatro Colón. In November of that year he made his debut with the San Francisco Opera Company. After 1951 he became a member of the Metropolitan Opera. Guest appearances and concert tours brought him great fame all over the world. In 1960 he toured the Soviet Union and in 1961-62 he went to Germany.

I heard Mr. Del Monaco in 1962 at the San Francisco Opera House. It was an October 13 performance of *I Pagliacci*, with Horne and Bastianini in the other major roles.

Del Monaco had a powerful voice with a glowing brightness in the high register. He also was a handsome man, and one of the greatest heroic tenors of his time.

Some of the best lyric-dramatic tenors of the Del Monaco era were: Bjoerling, Peerce, Di Stefano, Bergonzi, Gedda, and Kraus. And over the years, the heroic, dramatic tenors most like Del Monaco were: Caruso, Gigli, Martinelli, Melchior, Vinay, Tucker, Corelli, Vickers, and McCracken.

Beniamino Gigli
in *L'Africaine*

# BENIAMINO GIGLI

Beniamino Gigli, tenor, was born in Recanati, Italy, on March 20, 1890, and died in Rome on November 30, 1957.

He first worked in a pharmacy, and studied singing in off hours with Lazzarini in Recanati. After winning a scholarship in 1911 to the Accademia di Santa Cecilia in Rome, he became a pupil of the great teachers of the day, Antonio Cotogni and Enrico Rosati.

He made his debut in 1914 at Rovigo, Italy, as Enzo in *La Gioconda*. He then sang in Madrid, Barcelona, Paris, and Berlin before Toscanini brought him to La Scala, where he made an absolutely sensational debut as Faust in *Mefistofele*.

In 1921 after the death of Enrico Caruso, Gigli came to the Metropolitan Opera. He made his debut in *Andrea Chénier*. He belonged to the Met from 1921 to 1931. After a period in Europe he returned to the Met in 1938 and 1939. Scarcely any singer except Caruso has had a more lasting world fame. There was hardly an opera stage of world rank which was not the scene of his great triumphs.

Gigli was the greatest tenor I heard in my lifetime. I was not privileged to hear Caruso in person, although I have most of his recordings, but I did hear Gigli in person and after him all of the great tenors since Caruso. Judgment about Gigli comes without reservations. In his lifetime and mine he was up against almost unbelievable competition with the great tenors of the world rank, such as Martinelli, Lauri-Volpi, Pertile, McCormack, Fleta, Tauber, Schipa, and Melchior.

I have been asked how I would compare Gigli with more recent tenors such as: Bjoerling, Del Monaco, Tucker, Di Stefano, Corelli, Bergonzi, Pavarotti, and Domingo. My response is that in my opinion Gigli comes out number one. He had a combination of power, range, and beauty of voice not quite matched by any tenor since Caruso.

I shall never forget my attendance at one of Gigli's concerts in 1938, after he had quarreled with the Met, gone to Europe, and then returned to the U.S.A. He seemed determined to show Americans that between 1932 and 1938 we had lost the services of perhaps the greatest tenor on earth. His leaving the Met was during the depression when General Manager Gatti-Casazza asked all the singers to take a 10% cut in salary "to save the Metropolitan." Gigli, behind the scenes, it was reported, told Gatti that he would take a 10% cut in salary if Gatti did. Gatti apparently would not, so Gigli was off to Europe.

Now for that October 19, 1938 concert in Seattle. Gigli, determined to continue to win back the affections of the American people, "let out all the stops." I don't think that he ever sang better. Some of his great arias were: "O Paradiso" from *L'Africaine*, "M'appari" from *Marta*, "Vesti la giubba" from *I Pagliacci*, "la donna e mobile" from *Rigoletto*, "Che gelida manina" from *La Bohme*, "Celeste Ada" from *Ada*, and many of the great Italian folk songs, such as "oi mari, oi mari," "Torna a Surriento," "Core Ngrato," "Marechiare," and "O Sole Mio."

The willingness to sing "O Sole Mio" came as a result of my going back stage at intermission time. I slipped away from my wife, Marguerite, and her mother, Mrs. Perkins, hoping that the stage attendants would let me speak to Mr. Gigli while he was relaxing before the second half of his program. I finally talked my way to Mr. Gigli's quarters. He greeted me warmly. Then he asked me what singers I had heard before. After I told him he said, "You have heard some of the greatest in the world. What would you like me to sing as my encore?" I said "O Sole Mio." He sang it in that glorious manner accustomed to him. The crowd that had been giving him standing ovations most of the evening became almost delirious in a demonstration the like of which I had never witnessed before or since.

His accompanist was Maestro Rainaldo Zamboni.

# JAN KIEPURA

Jan Kiepura, tenor, was born on May 16, 1902, in Poland, and died on August 15, 1966, in Harrison, New York. He first studied politics and economics then voice in Warsaw with Tadeusz Leliva. He made his opera debut in 1924 in Lvov in *Faust*. After he had sung at the opera houses in Warsaw and Posnan, he appeared with brilliant success at the Vienna State Opera. He remained in that great house until 1928.

Mr. Kiepura had unusual success as a guest at the opera houses in Milan (La Scala), the Opera Comique, the Berlin State Opera, the Teatro Colón, and the Chicago Opera.

In the 1930s he made a number of outstanding films, both in Germany and in Hollywood. He often appeared in films with his wife, the soprano Marta Eggerth, whom he married in 1936.

Jan Kiepura made his debut as Rodolfo in *La Bohème* at the Metropolitan Opera. He sang there between 1938 and 1942. He also appeared frequently at other U.S.A. opera houses, in operettas, and in more films. He once appeared for over a year on Broadway in a production of *The Merry Widow*.

I heard Mr. Kiepura in concert in Seattle in 1939 at the Moore Theatre. He was in great voice. The audience called for one encore after another. There was a hint of Gigli in him, especially in Flotow's *M'Appari*. Other arias sung by him that evening were: "Questa o quella," "Che gelida manina," "Di quella pira," "Recondita armonia," "E lucevan le stelle," and "Celeste Aïda." Another number that brought down the house was "Be Mine Tonight" from his film of the same name.

I have been told that Mr. Kiepura could be difficult at times with impresarios, managers, and colleagues. However that may have been, it must be stated that Jan Kiepura had a glorious voice – one of the finest of his time.

# CHARLES KULLMAN

Charles Kullman, tenor, was born on January 13, 1903, in New Haven, Conn.

He started his singing lessons at the Juilliard School of Music in New York. He then took additional instruction at the American Conservatory at Fontainebleau before making his debut in 1929 with the American Opera Company. He joined this company for a two-year tour.

Mr. Kullman went to the Kroll Opera Company in 1931 and from there to the Berlin State Opera from 1932-36. He had simultaneous membership in the Vienna State Opera from 1934-36. He appeared at the Salzburg Festivals and at Covent Garden in London between 1934 and 1936. Upon his immediate return to the United States he was signed to a contract at the Met to make his debut in Gounod's opera *Faust*. He remained a leading tenor at the Metropolitan Opera until 1956.

Charles Kullman was also much in demand in Seattle, San Francisco, Chicago, Los Angeles, and elsewhere, while appearing in several films in Germany and the U.S.A.

Since he was a graduate of Yale University and had both high intelligence and singing experience, he obtained in 1956 a position on the Indiana University School of Music Faculty. There he served for many years as a singing teacher.

I heard Mr. Kullman a number of times on national radio broadcasts between 1935-1938. Then, in the season of 1946, the San Francisco Opera Company came to Seattle on tour. He sang Rodolfo to Dorothy Kirsten's Mimi in a marvelous production of *La Bohme*.

Charles Kullman had a fine tenor voice with brilliant timbre and a flexibility of delivery. With the international exposure that Mr. Kullman had, it seems strange that he did not receive the world-wide fame and acclaim he deserved.

Another outstanding American tenor voice of earlier years not acclaimed much anymore, belonged to Charles Hackett. He performed famously for many years at the Chicago Opera and the Metropolitan Opera.

Other American tenors, in my opinion, who never quite received their due at the Metropolitan and elsewhere, were Eugene Conley, Frederick Jagel, and Brian Sullivan.

James Melton, American tenor, who sang at the Metropolitan, considerably on the radio and in motion pictures, was a contemporary of Charles Kullman.

While Mr. Melton was handsome and had a very engaging personality, I never considered him a great singer. To me, he had a fine tenor voice that was more suited to light opera, Broadway productions, and the movies, than to grand opera, except in several very lyric roles. I heard Mr. Melton twice in person. He gave everything he had to the performances and in the lighter songs and lyric arias he was very well received.

# GIOVANNI MARTINELLI

Giovanni Martinelli, tenor, was born on October 22, 1885, in Montagnana, Italy, and died February 2, 1969, in New York.

During military service Mr. Martinelli was a clarinetist in a military band. The band leader was very "taken" with his vocal talents and, with his encouragement, Martinelli studied singing with Maestro Mandolini in Milan.

He made his debut in 1911 at the Teatro dal Verme, singing the title role in *Ernani*. His reputation developed very rapidly. In 1912 Toscanini chose him for the role of Dick Johnson in the La Scala premier of *La Fanciulla del West*. Also in 1912 he had a sensational success at Covent Garden.

In 1913 Mr. Martinelli was engaged by the Metropolitan Opera. He remained there until 1946 as one of that company's most esteemed tenors. He sang in Monte Carlo and in all the principal European musical centers.

Martinelli's singing of *Otello* at Covent Garden during the coronation season of 1937 was one of the most memorable for that famous "House." Also, Martinelli and Tibbett were a great team in *Otello* at the Metropolitan Opera.

I heard Martinelli in Seattle on April 3, 1930, in Meany Hall at the University of Washington. Among other arias he sang "O, Paradiso" from *L' Africaine*, "Vesti la giubba" from *Pagliacci*, "Che gelida manina" from *La Bohme*, "Di quella pira" from *Il Trovatore*, and "Amor ti vieta" from *Fedora*. His pianist was Giuseppe Bamboschek.

Martinelli had a voluminous voice of passionate quality. He was outstanding particularly in the heroic roles of Italian opera. After the death of Enrico Caruso, Martinelli and Gigli were generally considered by critics to be the legitimate successors to Caruso, particularly in the heroic roles of Italian opera.

Of these two world-famous, big voiced, dramatic tenors, Gigli's voice seemed to me the more beautiful.

# JOHN McCORMACK

John McCormack, lyric tenor, was born on June 14, 1884, in Athlone, Ireland, and died on September 16, 1945 in Dublin.

He began his vocal studies with Vincent O'Brien in Dublin and in 1902 won a singing contest there. In 1904 he had the privilege of singing at the World Exposition in St. Louis. He then went to Milan, Italy, and studied with Vincenzo Sabatini. His first opera appearance was in Savona, Italy, as the hero in *L'Amico Fritz*.

In 1906 Mr. McCormack gave successful concerts in London, and in 1907 he sang for the first time at Covent Garden, as Turiddu in *Cavalleria Rusticana*. He continued his triumphs at Covent Garden by singing there annually until 1914.

Mr. McCormack first launched his opera career in the United States at the Manhattan Opera House in New York in 1909. In 1910 he belonged to the Chicago-Philadelphia Opera Company. In the same year he made his debut at the Metropolitan Opera, of which he was a member from 1912-1914 and 1917-1918.

It was really in 1912 that Mr. McCormack began the long concert tours that over the years took him to every national and international music center. Everywhere he went he was greatly celebrated in the concert halls. Toward the end of his career he appeared rarely on the operatic stage. He did sing, however, in opera at Monte Carlo in 1921 and 1923. In 1938 Mr. McCormack gave his farewell concert in London. He lived thereafter in Ireland.

Mr. McCormack was regarded as one of the most famous tenors of his time – not opera tenors. Like John Charles Thomas, the great baritone, Mr. McCormack largely gained his world-wide recognition from his many concert appearances, and great "out-put" of recordings. The years that he did spend in opera were in lyric roles, and on the concert stage he thrilled millions with Irish songs.

Mr. McCormack was a wealthy man, not because of birth but because his beautiful voice made millions of dollars for him. Mr. Caruso and Mr. McCormack were fine friends, and they would very often engage in pleasantries. One year when Mr. McCormack's record sales were greater than that of Mr. Caruso's the Italian tenor said, "John, that is all right for this year, but don't let it happen again." On another occasion when the two met, Mr. McCormack said to Mr. Caruso, "How is the world's greatest tenor today?" Caruso replied, "Since when did you become a baritone?"

John McCormack had the finest lyric tenor voice I ever heard, followed closely by Tito Schipa in his prime, Richard Tauber, and the great American tenor Richard Crooks.

Mr. McCormack's voice was one of exquisite tonal quality. He could sing a gorgeous high B-flat and in his early years, a high C by going into what is called a "head-tone." Some authorities said that Mr. McCormack was using falsetto. No one knew for sure, but the voice change was so imperceptible and ravishingly beautiful that few cared how the tone was produced.

For me, Mr. McCormack's voice was more beautiful when I heard him in person and saw his movie *Song o' My Heart* than when I listened to many of his records, great as they were. In person, his voice seemed larger, broader, more expansive – and, more beautiful.

I heard Mr. McCormack at the Fox Theatre in Seattle on Monday evening, January 18, 1932. Edwin Schneider was at the piano. Mr. McCormack began his program by singing "O Sleep, Why Dost Thou Leave Me?" by *Handel*.

He then launched into the great heart appeal songs: "Kathleen Mavourneen," "Just for Today," "The Rose of Tralee," "Then You'll Remember Me," "Macushla," and "I Hear you Calling Me." Most of the time, while he was singing, the theater was dark, except for the spotlight on him. When the lights came on, all over the theater there was hardly a dry eye in the audience, even among the men. It was an incredible performance.

John McCormack, by documented evidence, was the greatest concert attraction in history.

Lauritz Melchior as
Sigfried

# LAURITZ MELCHIOR

Lauritz Melchior, tenor, was born on March 20, 1890, in Copenhagen.

He took singing lessons in 1908 with Paul Bang in Copenhagen and made his debut as a baritone in 1913 in the role of Silvio in *I Pagliacci* at the Royal Opera in Copenhagen. During his engagements there, in 1917-18 he studied with Vilhelm Herold. Beginning in 1918 he sang tenor roles.

Mr. Melchior remained at the Copenhagen Opera until 1921 and often appeared there later as a guest artist. He continued his vocal studies with Victor Beigel in London, Ernst Grenzebach in Berlin, and Anna Bahr-Mildenburg in Munich. In 1924, he appeared with great success at Covent Garden. Thereafter he was an annual guest in London. He was the chief tenor at the Bayreuth Festivals from 1924-31. He was regarded as the greatest Wagner tenor of his time and perhaps of all time.

Mr. Melchior was on the roster of the Berlin State Opera from 1935-39. He also appeared in guest roles in Vienna, Munich, Paris, Brussels, Milan, Stockholm, Chicago, and San Francisco. In 1926 he appeared at the Metropolitan, making his debut in *Tannhäuser*. From then on he experienced triumph after triumph at the Met until he left there in 1950. After 1949 he appeared in Hollywood films. With the giving-up of his operatic career, he appeared in operettas, musicals, and revues. He had the ideal qualities of the heroic tenor: the baritone warmth, the big voice, and the tenor range. His Wagner roles were absolutely unmatchable – and still are to this day.

I heard Mr. Melchior in San Francisco in 1939 in the opera *Tristan and Isolde*, with three other opera greats in the cast – Flagstad, Meisle, and Kipnis.

Mr. Melchior was at the height of his powers in 1939. With the giant San Francisco Opera Orchestra, under the able conductor McArthur, this Wagner staple was a huge success.

Jan Peerce as Rodolfo
in *La Bohème*

# JAN PEERCE

Jan Peerce, tenor, was born June 3, 1904, in New York. He sang as a boy in a synagogue in New York. He then studied the violin and worked as a violinist and singer in a night club.

From 1933-38 he sang concert songs on the radio and at the Radio City Music Hall, with considerable beauty of voice. His first appearance in opera was in Philadelphia in 1938. In 1940 the Metropolitan Opera engaged him to make his debut as Alfredo in *La Traviata* From there he had one success after another. Arturo Toscanini, famed conductor, was so fond of Peerce's voice that he engaged him to sing in the Toscanini opera productions the maestro presented on the radio in 1944-45.

The two became good friends and on several occasions Mr. Toscanini referred to Mr. Peerce as his "favorite tenor." In jest, one time, while visiting with Mr. Peerce, Toscanini was quoted as saying, "Jan, I am told that you are Jewish. That is hard for me to believe because you sound in your singing so much like an Italian—with the sob in your voice and other Italian characteristics." It is said Jan Peerce responded, "Maestro, I am Jewish. I remember my father and mother and my grandparents, on both sides, and they were all Jewish. Beyond that, of course, I don't know." Toscanini, in good humor, replied, "Jan, that is where the Italian comes in."

Peerce appeared as guest in San Francisco, Chicago, Los Angeles, and South America with brilliant success. He was the first American singer to appear at the Bolshoi Theatre (1955). Concert tours took him to Australia, New Zealand, Austria, South Africa, Sweden, Japan, and all over the U.S.A. Mr. Peerce had a very beautiful, steady, expressive voice and was at his best in French and Italian opera.

I heard Mr. Peerce in Seattle with the San Francisco Opera Company in its 1946 season. Licia Albanese was the Violetta to his Alfredo in *La Traviata*. It was a memorable occasion, with much favorable buzzing by the audience at intermission time. I heard him both in opera and concert several times later.

He went on to become one of America's greatest tenors. He had a very distinguished career at the Metropolitan and all over the world. He was also a much loved person, especially by younger singers whom he helped with their careers, such as Roberta Peters, and other well-known persons.

# TITO SCHIPA

Tito Schipa, lyric tenor, was born on January 2, 1889, in Lecce, Italy, and died December 16, 1965 in New York City.

He began his vocal studies with Alceste Gerunda in Lecce, Italy, and continued with Emilio Piccoli in Milan.

He made his debut in 1911 in Vercelli, Italy, and sang on small stages for several years. In 1913 he sang at the Teatro Colón and at the Opera in Rio de Janeiro. Then, in 1915, he made his debut at La Scala as Vladimir in *Prince Igor*. On March 27, 1917, he created the role of Ruggiero in the world premier of *La Rondine* at Monte Carlo.

His world fame really began at the Chicago Opera where he sang from 1919-32. After 1927 he regularly sang in South America, and of course, in Chicago. He made his debut at the Metropolitan in 1933, where he sang until 1935, and then again in 1940-41. His debut at the Met was as Nemorino in *L'Elisir d' Amore*. After leaving the Met in 1941, he returned again to the Teatro Colón. Then he went on to Russia, where he sang in Moscow, Leningrad, and Riga. Even at the age of 70 he was still giving concerts.

Mr. Schipa was the first great singer with an international reputation that I ever heard in person. He was to sing at the Metropolitan Theatre in Seattle on Monday evening, March 14, 1927. On "scraping-up" the necessary $1.00 and with the encouragement of my high school English teacher (Anna Burns), I went to hear Mr. Schipa. His accompanist was Maestro José Enchaniz.

I could not believe the beauty of Mr. Schipa's voice. It was a lyric voice with a velvety melodic line; and he sang with the least effort of any of the great male singers I have heard from that time until now. The power of his voice, while not great in comparison to a number of dramatic tenors I have heard since, was certainly big enough to fill the auditorium with the gorgeous tones he emitted. Two of the arias he sang that evening were composed by Massenet: "Ah, fuyez douce image" from *Manon*, and the "Ossian Song" from *Werther*. Mixed with other opera arias were beautiful

62

songs such as "Granada," "Liebestraum," "Torna A Surriento," and "O Sole Mio." In later years I heard him again in both opera and concert.

Along with other lyric tenors of great renown, such as McCormack, Tauber, Crooks, Tagliavini, and Valletti, Mr. Schipa left a legacy of singing as a bel canto lyric tenor. In my opinion, in his prime Mr. Schipa was one of the two or three greatest lyric tenors of all time.

# RICHARD TUCKER

Richard Tucker, tenor, was born on August 28, 1913, in Brooklyn, New York, and died on January 8, 1975.

He sang in the choir of a New York synagogue at the age of six. He later studied with tenor Paul Althouse. He made his concert debut in New York in 1944 and his opera debut at the Metropolitan in 1945, as Enzo in *La Gioconda*. Very soon thereafter he was highly successful in a radio broadcast, as Radames in *Aïda*, directed by Arturo Toscanini. In all, he was a member of the Metropolitan Opera for almost thirty years, with great success.

In 1947 at the Arena Festival, he sang Enzo in *La Gioconda* opposite Maria Callas, and both singers were greatly applauded. He was immediately signed to appear at La Scala and sang there as a guest artist. In 1958 he made guest appearances at Covent Garden and in Vienna.

Further opera appearances took him to San Francisco, Seattle, Los Angeles, and Chicago. Everywhere he was given great ovations, not only in opera but also in concert tours in Italy, Israel, and throughout North and South America.

I heard Mr. Tucker (1965) in San Francisco in the War Memorial Opera House in the Opera *Andrea Chénier*, in a cast with Renata Tebaldi and Ettore Bastianini. The conductor was Molinari-Pradelli. I could not believe the size and beauty of Tucker's voice. I had heard Gigli and Martinelli both in their prime, both with extremely large voices, but I could not take in what I was hearing. Tucker's voice was as big as theirs. I had heard many of his recordings, but that is different from hearing a voice in a big opera house. I do believe, however, that Gigli had a slight edge in beauty of voice over both Martinelli and Tucker.

One of the most taxing arias in *Andrea Chénier* is "Un di all' azzurro spazio." Mr. Tucker's breath control, coupled with the size and beauty of his voice, provoked a prolonged standing ovation after the aria.

Richard Tucker was a wonderful family man. I shall never forget the evening Mrs. Blair and I met Sara, Richard, and their two sons after a

Richard Tucker
in *Don Carlo*

performance. The great regard they had for each other was immediately evident.

The great baritone Robert Merrill, who probably sang more with Richard Tucker than any other singer and who had many other tenor partners, said at the time of Tucker's death, "He was the greatest tenor in the world." Rudolf Bing, with other compliments said, "He is irreplaceable." My own opinion, after having heard Richard Tucker a number of times, is that between about 1955 and 1967 he was the greatest tenor in the world. That world, at the time, included such lyric-dramatic tenors as Del Monaco, Di Stefano, Peerce, Vickers, Tagliavini, Bergonzi, Valletti, Kraus, Gedda, and McCracken. Corelli was there, also. He will be discussed separately elsewhere in this book.

In Richard Tucker's era there also was the tenor Mario Lanza. He was heard most often in the movies, on recordings, and in concerts – rarely ever, in complete operas. It is unquestionable that he had a great and glorious voice.

# MEZZO-SOPRANOS

Marilyn Horne as Adalgisa
in *Norma*

# MARILYN HORNE

Marilyn Horne, mezzo-soprano, was born in 1934 in Bradford, Pa. She studied at the University of Southern California and with William Vennard in Los Angeles. She made her debut as Hata in the *Bartered Bride* with the Los Angeles Guild Opera in 1954. Shortly thereafter, she was engaged as a concert singer. In 1954 she sang for the film star Dorothy Dandridge in the film *Carmen Jones*.

In 1956 Miss Horne went to Europe, where she was engaged at Gelsenkirchen from 1956-59. During that time she was greatly applauded as guest in Vienna, Venice, and Germany. In 1960 she returned to the United States and starred in *Wozzeck* and other operas in San Francisco and the Chicago Opera. In 1964 she had great triumphs at Covent Garden and at the Edinburgh Festival. In the concert halls she appears frequently with Joan Sutherland.

In the spring of 1962 in San Francisco I heard Miss Horne as Rosina in the *Barber of Seville*. Some of her colleagues were Manton, Fredricks, Beattie, and Macurdy. The conductor was Kritz. The audience gave Miss Horne a tremendous ovation.

Since I heard Miss Horne, she has appeared in most of the major opera houses in the United States, including the Metropolitan, in Canada, and all over Europe, including La Scala.

Miss Horne is one of the best singers in the world today. She has a great range, singing both soprano and mezzo roles. She possesses a very beautiful voice with considerable power. Also, as a musician, she has few equals.

I consider Miss Horne at the top among present day mezzo-sopranos.

Regina Resnik as Klytämnestra
in *Elektra*

## REGINA RESNIK

Regina Resnik, soprano-contralto, was born on August 30, 1923, in New York.

At Harvard University she studied voice with Fritz Busch and won a prize in the Metropolitan Opera Auditions of the Air contest. In 1942 she made her opera debut at the New York City Opera as Santuzza in *Cavalleria Rusticana*.

In 1943 Miss Resnik sang at the Mexico City Opera and in 1945 she was given a contract to join the Metropolitan Opera. There, in 1948, she sang Ellen Orford in the first New York performance of *Peter Grimes*. She then made guest appearances in Chicago, San Francisco, London, and Paris. In 1953 she sang Sieglinde in *Die Walküre* at the Bayreuth Festival. At this time her voice changed to mezzo-soprano and, after further study with the baritone Giuseppe Danise, she appeared at the Metropolitan Opera in 1956 as Marina in *Boris Godounov*.

In 1957 she had outstanding successes at Covent Garden. Beginning in 1958 she appeared often at the Vienna State Opera. In 1960 she was acclaimed at the Salzburg Festival as Eboli in *Don Carlos*. That same year she appeared at Bayreuth as Fricka in the *Ring Cycle*. After that, she made guest appearances at the Teatro Colón and at the major Italian opera houses, including La Scala.

I heard Miss Resnik in San Francisco when she appeared as Carmen. This was in 1964. Other members of the cast were: Costa, Martell, and Hecht. The conductor was Prêtre.

Miss Resnik was a great Carmen. She had a big voice of dark tonal quality and was a fine actress. At the time I heard her she was the reigning Carmen at the Metropolitan.

# ERNESTINE SCHUMANN-HEINK

Ernestine Schumann-Heink, mezzo-soprano, was born June 15, 1861, in Lieben, Germany, and died November 17, 1936, in Hollywood, California. She studied singing with Mariette von Leclair in Graz. At the age of fifteen she sang the mezzo-soprano solo in *Beethoven's Ninth Symphony* in Graz.

Miss Schumann-Heink made her opera debut in 1878 at the Dresden Royal Opera in *Il Trovatore*, as Azucena. In 1882 she came to the Kroll Opera and in 1883 to the Hamburg Opera, where she sang for sixteen years.

Under Gustav Mahler in 1892 she appeared at Covent Garden with brilliant success in a production of the Ring Cycle. In 1898 she sang in Chicago, her first appearance in the United States. In 1899 she was engaged by the Metropolitan Opera, making her debut as Ortrud in *Lohengrin*. She sang there until 1932. Miss Schumann-Heink's opera triumphs in the U.S.A. were almost always in German operas. She did, however, in 1935, make a highly successful American film entitled, "Here's to Romance." She was generally considered to be the most famous mezzo-soprano of her generation. Another mezzo-soprano of Miss Schumann-Heink's era, was the famous American lady, Louise Homer.

I heard Miss Schumann-Heink in person at the Fox Theatre in Seattle in 1930. Although she was nearing the end of her career, her voice was big, steady, and beautiful. One of her encores – "Silent Night! Holy Night!" was sung in German, to thunderous applause.

## GIULIETTA SIMIONATO

Giulietta Simionato, mezzo-soprano, was born on December 15, 1910, in Forli, Italy. She spent her childhood in Sardinia and studied voice in Rovigo with Ettore Lucatello and in Milan with Guido Palumbo.

In Florence, in 1933, she won a singing contest and made her opera debut there in *L'Orseolo* in 1938. By 1939 she was singing at La Scala, where for more than twenty years she was a principal mezzo-soprano.

In 1942, Miss Simionato also had a phenomenal success at La Scala as Rosina in the *Barber of Seville*. After World War II she sang in opera all over the world. For example, Miss Simionato sang at Covent Garden, the Teatro Colón, the Paris Opera, the New York City Opera, and the State operas in Munich and Berlin. In addition, she sang in the opera houses in Brussels, Chicago, Mexico City, and Rio de Janeiro. To somewhat complete the list, Miss Simionato sang at the Vienna State Opera, at the Arena, Edinburgh, Maggio Musicale, the Holland Festivals, the Salzburg Festivals and in San Francisco. In 1959 she made her debut at the Metropolitan Opera as Azucena in a sensational performance. At that House she gave a number of other memorable performances. She gave up her stage career in 1966.

I heard Miss Simionato in 1962 at the San Francisco Opera House in *Verdi's Il Trovatore*. With her in the cast were Ross, McCracken, Bastianini, and Hecht. Molinari-Pradelli conducted. Miss Simionato's Azucena demonstrated a big, ravishing voice; and her acting was superb. Later on in San Francisco that same year 1962, Miss Simionato had a tremendous success as Santuzza in *Cavalleria Rusticana*. Her rendition of the aria "Voi lo sapete" received a thunderous applause.

Besides beauty of voice and volume for a mezzo-soprano, Miss Simionato had a great range. That made it possible for her to be so successful even in soprano roles. A case in point was her Rosina, in the *Barber of Seville* in San Francisco in 1953, in a cast that included Valletti, Guarrera, Baccaloni, and Rossi-Lemeni, with Serafin conducting. The newspapers extolled Miss Simionato greatly in this typically soprano role, especially her rendition of "Una Voce Poco Fa." There is no question but that Miss Simionato was one of the finest mezzo-sopranos of our time. I

Giulietta Simionato as Santuzza
in *Cavalleria Rusticana*

have found that she was not only a world renowned singer but a woman of much compassion. I knew that she and the late Ettore Bastianini were partners in many operas and very good friends. In fact, I heard them both in operas a number of times. Since I was such an admirer of the great Bastianini, I wrote to Miss Simionato several times to her home in Rome, Italy. I had in mind, perhaps, writing a book about Bastianini. We exchanged a number of letters. I wrote to her in English and she responded in Italian. We both had our interpreters so that the nuances of the letters would not be lost.

In 1978-79 Mrs. Blair and I made a European trip and while we were in Rome, I contacted Miss Simionato, who in turn put me in touch with her dear friend Rita Koch, whose residence was in Vienna. Miss Simionato's idea, of course, was that because Miss Koch spoke and wrote such excellent English, she would be an invaluable asset in any book that I might write about Bastianini. Miss Koch knew Bastianini well and when I visited with her on the telephone while we were in Vienna, she offered to take us to Siena, Italy, Bastianini's birthplace and home so that we could visit with his relatives and friends who knew him and loved him so much. Miss Koch was a very intelligent, pleasant and professional lady.

The purpose in my writing this information additional to my remarks regarding the vocal career of Miss Simionato is to speak about her character. In all her comments about Bastianini and people in general, one could see a warm, compassionate person—one who really cares about people. That attribute, combined with a great singing voice, makes Giulietta Simionato an unusual person.

Risë Stevens as
Carmen

# RISË STEVENS

Risë Stevens, mezzo-soprano, was born June 11, 1913, in New York. She sang on the radio when she was very young, and then took her vocal studies at the Juilliard School of Music in New York. In 1935 she went to Europe and studied in Vienna with Marie Gutheil-Schoder and Herbert Graf.

Miss Stevens made her debut in 1936 at the Opera in Prague as Mignon. She stayed in Prague until 1938. During those years she sang Octavian in *Der Rosenkavalier* at the Vienna State Opera. She also took the same role that year at the Teatro Colón. In 1939 she was well received at the Glyndebourne Festival as Cherubino in *Le Nozze di Figaro*. Also in 1939 she made her debut at the Metropolitan Opera as Mignon.

Miss Stevens remained a member of the Metropolitan as a principal mezzo-soprano for more than twenty years. In 1940 she had a great triumph there as Cherubino. She appeared as guest in Europe, singing in Paris and London. In 1956 she was applauded as an unforgettable Orphée in Gluck's Opera at the Festival of the Acropolis in Athens. After Miss Stevens bade her farewell to the Metropolitan in 1964, she became the leader of the Metropolitan National Opera Company, a traveling troupe.

I heard Miss Stevens in San Francisco in 1940 in the War Memorial Opera House as Cherubino in *The Marriage of Figaro*. Also in the cast were Sayão, Rethberg, Pinza, and Brownlee. Leinsdorf was the conductor. It was an outstanding production

Miss Stevens was a very attractive, vivacious lady with a voluminous, rich, and expressive voice. She was a fine actress also. Perhaps two of her best roles were as Carmen and Orphée. She was certainly one of the outstanding opera singers of her time. Some fine mezzo-sopranos of her era were Swarthout, Stignani, Castagna, Simionato, Resnik, Barbieri, Thorborg, Thebom, Rankin, Merriman, Dalis, Elias, Conner, and Ludwig.

The opera world still remembers and loves Risë Stevens.

# EBE STIGNANI

Ebe Stignani, mezzo-soprano, was born on July 11, 1904, in Naples. In Naples she studied voice at the Conservatory of San Pietro a Majella with Agostino Roche. The director of the San Carlo Opera Company heard her at a school performance and hired her for his company, where in 1925 she made her debut as Amneris in *Ada*.

Toscanini soon heard her and engaged her for La Scala. Her debut there was as Eboli in *Don Carlos*. She remained the principal mezzo-soprano at La Scala until 1953. In 1927 Miss Stignani first appeared at the Teatro ColÂn and in 1938 was greatly applauded as Amneris at Covent Garden. At the Maggio Musicale Festival in 1940 she sang the coloratura mezzo-soprano part of Arsaces in *Semiramide*. This great artist had an absolutely fantastic reception in Europe and South America but made surprisingly few appearances in the United States. She did, however, have concerts in Minneapolis and New York City and sang in opera in San Francisco.

It is hard to believe, but true, that Miss Stignani was never offered a contract at the Metropolitan Opera. She told friends that this inattention by the Met was one of the great sorrows of her life.

Mrs. Blair and I heard Miss Stignani at the San Francisco Opera House during the 1938-39 season. Miss Stignani's role was that of Santuzza in *Cavalleria Rusticana*. Some other members of the cast were Ziliani, Tagliabue, and Votipka. The conductor was Gaetano Merola.

Miss Stignani had a fabulous voice. She was not much of an actress, but the glorious tones that she produced were compensation enough. In the last years of her career, she sang principally on the larger Italian stages.

During her world-wide career, some of the mezzo-sopranos who most nearly approached Miss Stignani as a vocalist were: Schuman-Heink, Homer, Castagna, Thorborg, Anderson, Swarthout, Stevens, Resnik, Simionato, Barbieri, Ludwig, Thebom, Cossotto, Horne, Gorr, Elmo, and Pederzini.

Other mezzo-sopranos who have or are making their mark on the world scene include: Bumbry, Verrett, Elias, Berganza, Dalis, Pirazzini, Dominguez, Tourangeau, Amparan, Baltsa, Obratsova, Troyanos, and Von Stade.

# GLADYS SWARTHOUT

Gladys Swarthout, mezzo-soprano, was born on December 25, 1904, in Deepwater, Missouri, and died, July 7, 1969, in Florence, Italy. She sang in church concerts when she was only thirteen years of age. After her study at the Bush Conservatory in Chicago, she made her debut at the opera there in 1924 as the Shepherd Boy in *Tosca*. For a time she sang only smaller roles in Chicago, but in 1925 she received the opportunity to sing Carmen in nearby Ravinia at the Summer Opera.

The Metropolitan in 1929 engaged Miss Swarthout to sing La Cieca in *La Gioconda*. She remained at the Metropolitan until 1945 as a principal member of the company. Two of her best roles at the Met were as Carmen and Mignon. In 1934 she appeared at the Metropolitan in the world premiere of *Merry Mount* with Lawrence Tibbett. She also had great success in films such as *Champagne Waltz*. In 1932 she was married to baritone Frank Chapman.

Guest appearances took Miss Swarthout to such places as San Francisco, Chicago, London, and Paris, all with great acclaim. After 1940 she gave the majority of her time to concert singing. In 1954 she had a severe heart attack, which caused her to retire from musical life.

Miss Swarthout was a lovely woman and person with a great voice. I heard her in San Francisco as *Carmen* during the 1940-41 opera season. Other members of the cast were Albanese, Jobin, Weede, and Cehanovsky. Leinsdorf was the conductor. Miss Swarthout, in the title role, took the audience by storm. All through her career she was dearly loved. Between 1934 and 1946 millions of people heard her on national radio broadcasts.

Miss Swarthout, along with Risë Stevens and Regina Resnik, were three of America's greatest mezzo-sopranos. Their international reputation was immense also.

# BARITONES

## ETTORE BASTIANINI

Ettore Bastianini, baritone, was born in Siena, Italy, on September 24, 1922, and died in Sirmione, Italy, on January 25, 1967. He made his debut as a bass in 1945 at Ravenna as Colline in *La Bohme*. He successfully sang bass parts for several years but was changed into a baritone by his teacher, Rucciana Betarini. He made his debut as a baritone in 1951. He was much admired when he sang Prince Andrei in *War and Peace* at the 1953 Maggio Musicale Festival. He first sang at La Scala in 1953 and later became the absolute King of Baritones there.

In December of 1953 he made his debut at the Metropolitan Opera as the elder Germont in *La Traviata*. He was soon one of the best known and heralded of Italian baritones. He performed on all the great opera stages of the world. New York, Chicago, Milan, Vienna and San Francisco especially sought his services. There was also great clamor for him to appear in Salzburg, Germany, France, Spain, Egypt, and South America. He had a voice that was voluminous, vibrant, rich, dark, haunting, and passionate in quality. On entering the stage and before singing a note in opera roles, the audience would give him an ovation.

I heard Mr. Bastianini at the War Memorial Opera House in San Francisco, during that company's 1961-62 season. On October 20, 1961, he sang Renato in *Un Ballo in Maschera*, and on October 23 he had the lead role in *Nabucco*. Both operas were sensational. Mrs. Blair and I were so taken with the great Bastianini voice that we went to hear him as Count Di Luna in *Il Trovatore* on October 2, 1962, again in San Francisco. At the same House on October 13, 1962 he did one of the most memorable Tonio's in *I Pagliacii* I have ever heard. Sir Rudolf Bing in his book *A Knight at the Opera*, wrote, "Ettore Bastianini had one of the most beautiful baritone voices in my time." Also, Walter Price of the Metropolitan, in discussing Bastianini's role as Barnaba, wrote, "Ettore Bastianini brings back memories of Ruffo with the breadth of his range and power."

Bastianini died tragically in 1967 at age 43 with cancer of the vocal cords. I wrote to Giulietta Simionato, one of his dear friends and a partner in many Bastianini casts, to hear of his last days. I knew that Miss Simionato and her doctor-husband were in constant contact with the desperately ill Bastianini. After his death Miss Simionato wrote me that "Bastianini had the greatest baritone voice of her time, and that he was also a great human being." We shall all look forward to hearing the Bastianini voice in that better land where he is now singing with the angels.

Other opera roles of Bastianini were in *Rigoletto, Don Carlos, Lucia, Il Barbiere Di Siviglia, La Favorita,* and *La Bohème.* Also one wonders if his "Son sessant' anni" and "Nemico della Patria" from *Andrea Chénier* will ever be surpassed.

Bastianini's partners in the opera houses of the world and on recordings were very often: Callas, Tebaldi, Del Monaco, Simionato, Bergonzi, Di Stefano, Corelli, Bjoerling, Scotto, Cossotto, Stella, Vinco, Siepi, Corena, Poggi, and Kraus.

There is no question in my mind but that before his throat problems Bastianini had one of the greatest baritone voices of his time and perhaps of all time.

# IGOR GORIN

Igor Gorin, baritone, was born October 26, 1908, in Gradizhak, Russian Ukraine. His family moved to Vienna, where he studied medicine and sang in a medical school choral group.

Mr. Gorin began his serious musical studies at the Vienna Conservatory of Music, studies which extended from 1925-30. He made his vocal debut at the Vienna Volksoper. He sang at the Vienna and Czech State Operas and at a number of other opera houses.

After coming to the United States in 1933 Mr. Gorin sang in radio recitals prior to making his great concert debut at the Hollywood Bowl. That appearance gave him opportunities to sing with leading American symphony orchestras and to appear at a number of opera houses before he joined the Met.

After 1948 he sang annually the role of Brigham Young in *All Faces West*, the Mormon Pageant at Ogden, Utah. Among other opportunities, Mr. Gorin appeared as the elder Germont in *La Traviata* and as Rigoletto on N.B.C. television. In 1959 he gave concerts in Australia and New Zealand. His versatility included composing as well as singing in several motion pictures. He became an American citizen in 1939.

I heard Mr. Gorin in concert in Seattle in 1952, when he was at the height of his vocal powers. It was during the period when he was thrilling millions of people with his frequent radio appearances on the Telephone Hour and The Voice of Firestone.

That evening among other arias and songs, Mr. Gorin sang the following: "Prologue" from *I Pagliacci*, "Song to the Evening Star" from *Tannhäuser*, "Eri Tu" from *The Masked Ball* "Di Provenza" from *La Traviata*, "Vision Fugitive" from *Herodiade*, "The Blind Ploughman," "Sylvia," and "The Lord's Prayer."

Mr. Gorin combined a rich, warm voice and exceptional musicianship with an outstanding stage personality. The large audience thrilled to his crescendos from exquisite pianissimo to dynamic fortissimo.

During the 1963-64 season the Metropolitan Opera Company called Mr. Gorin to New York for his debut as the Elder Germont in *La Traviata*. The Cast included Beverly Sills and John Craig. Franco Patané conducted.

Cornell MacNeil as Rigoletto

# CORNELL MacNEIL

Cornell MacNeil, baritone, was born in Minneapolis, Minnesota, on September 24, 1922. In his early years he worked as a machinist and later studied singing at the Hartt School in Hartford, Connecticut. Following that experience, Mr. MacNeil took voice lessons from the great German baritone Friedrich Schorr.

Cornell MacNeil made his debut on March 1, 1950, in Philadelphia as John Sorel in the world premier of *The Consul*. He sang next with several small opera companies, soon making his debut with the New York Center Opera and performing there from 1952-55.

In 1955 he was applauded for his singing at the San Francisco Opera as the Herald in *Lohengrin* and as Sharpless in *Madame Butterfly*. In 1957 he made guest appearances in the opera houses of Caracas, Mexico City, and Chicago. La Scala then called him. He had a sensational success there in the opera *Ernani*. Since 1959 Mr. MacNeil has been a principal baritone at the Metropolitan Opera, making his debut as Rigoletto. Some of his other major roles have been in *Un Ballo in Maschera, Nabucco, Aïda, Cavalleria Rusticana, I Pagliaccci, Luisa Miller,* and *La Faniculla del West.*

I heard Mr. MacNeil in 1961 at the San Francisco Opera in *Rigoletto* with Renato Cioni and the lovely Mary Costa as Gilda. The conductor was Silvio Varviso. I have never heard the role of Rigoletto sung better. In that period Mr. MacNeil was at the height of his vocal powers, with a big, rich voice of outstanding range. I heard him later with the Seattle Opera Company as Scarpia in a highly successful production of *Tosca*.

Mr. MacNeil has long ranked high among American baritones and has achieved international distinction.

Robert Merrill as
Escamillo in *Carmen*

# ROBERT MERRILL

Robert Merrill, baritone, was born in New York in 1919. He completed his vocal studies in New York and then sang for various radio stations. He was hired by the Metropolitan Opera in 1945, made his debut as the elder Germont in a production of *La Traviata*, and appeared on that occasion with Licia Albanese and Richard Tucker. Since that time he has sung in San Francisco, Seattle, Chicago, London, South America, and many other places. At the Met he had a highly successful career as a principal baritone for more than 30 years. Mr. Merrill had won the Metropolitan Opera Auditions of the Air contest before his debut at the Met.

In 1945 he sang before both Houses of Congress at the memorial service for President Franklin Delano Roosevelt. Later Mr. Merrill was chosen by Arturo Toscanini to sing Germont and Renato in the famed conductor's radio broadcasts. He also made a motion picture in Hollywood.

Mr. Merrill had a voice of great warmth and volume. The critic Irving Kolodin, after Merrill's debut in New York's Met, said in part, "polished and powerful...noble endowment."

I have a special fondness for Robert Merrill. He is a class person. I first met him after a Seattle concert he gave shortly after his Met debut. I heard him again in 1959 when I was on the Concert's Board in Greeley, Colorado. We brought him to that city for a performance. He was always the same, very modest in his demeanor, warm, and personable. These traits he exhibited even after his great triumphs in the world's leading opera houses. I have heard him often.

In operas and on recordings, because of his great fame, Robert Merrill was partnered with the most important singers of his time, such as: Tebaldi, Price, Sutherland, Bjoerling, Tucker, Peerce, Corelli, and Bergonzi.

By a phenomenon of nature Mr. Merrill was singing better at age 50 than he did at age 40, as wonderful as his voice was then. The passing of the years made his voice bigger, freer, and ever more sumptuous, without loss of beauty. In the 1960s and into the 1970s, he was, in my opinion, the world's greatest baritone.

I have two beautiful letters from him which I prize highly. Starting with the middle 1960s, Sherrill Milnes – a singer of great consequence whom I have heard a number of times – became Merrill's chief competition. Mr. Milnes is a large, affable man, who learns roles easily, is a splendid musician, and actor, and has high tones that even tenors envy. He is at his absolute best in operas such as *Ernani*, *Macbeth*, and *La Forza Del Destino*, where he takes optional high notes.

In comparing the two men I would say that Mr. Merrill in his prime had the more thrilling voice. Through its entire range, the Merrill voice had the more beauty, body, and virility. Mr. Milnes' voice, of course, was and is a world-class voice. Probably no baritone is singing better in the world today.

Some other baritones presently making high marks in the world are: Cappuccilli, Wixell, Quilico, Bruson, Manuguerra, Elvíra, Nucci, Krause, Panerai, and Fischer-Dieskau.

# JOHN CHARLES THOMAS

John Charles Thomas, baritone, was born on September 6, 1891, in Meyersdale, Pennsylvania, and died in December of 1960 in New York. He was the son of a Methodist minister. He studied with Adelin Fermin in New York City and with the legendary tenor Jean de Reszke.

At first Thomas planned a medical career. But yearning to be involved in full-time music, he dropped out of medical school. On winning a scholarship to study music at the Peabody Conservatory in Baltimore, he was well on his way musically.

His first successes in his new profession were as an operetta singer in the works of Friml, Lehar, Romberg, Victor Herbert, and Gilbert and Sullivan. Extremely successful as an operetta singer and very highly paid, he nevertheless decided to go into grand opera.

He soon sang at the Brussels Opera and Covent Garden in England. Then, to great "raves" of publicity, he sang at the opera houses in Philadelphia, San Francisco, and Chicago. On February 2, 1934 he made his debut at the Metropolitan as Giorgio Germont in *La Traviata*, in a cast that included Tito Schipa and Rosa Ponselle.

About his debut in Chicago, as Tonio in *Pagliacci*, the critic reporting the event as produced by Rubini Records Gv910, had the following to say about Thomas. "He appeared without fanfare and literally took the house by storm, producing a demonstration unlike anything since Galli-Curci first sang at the Auditorium. His prologue was an absolute marvel and at the end of the first act shouts for Thomas went up all over the theater. Not even a solo bow by Charles Marshall (the Canio of the evening) could silence the crowd. 'Thomas!, Thomas!' the audience cried. Marshall brought out all the members of the cast, but Thomas would not appear alone. Still the audience was not satisfied. They wanted Thomas and spent the whole intermission, even with the house lights up, yelling his name."

Thomas' debut at the Met in *La Traviata* is well written in glowing terms by Irving Kolodin in his "History of the Metropolitan." Shortly after the death of Mr. Thomas in 1960, Frank Chapman, baritone and husband of Gladys Swarthout, writing for "Opera News," said that the four greatest

John Charles Thomas as Giorgio Germont
in *La Traviata*

singers he ever heard were Caruso, Ponselle, John Charles Thomas, and Pinza. Mr. Thomas had a baritone voice of great power and beauty with an unusual range and freedom in his upper register that produced glorious tones. As fine an opera career as Mr. Thomas had, it must be said that much of his fame came from his concerts, radio appearances, and his R.C.A. Victor recordings. R.C.A. Victor, in the early 1950s, produced a recording named "Ten Unforgotten Stars." They were: Bori, Caruso, de Luca, Galli-Curci, Gigli, McCormack, Ponselle, Schipa, Tibbett, and Thomas. Thus, with R.C.A.'s great stable of stars, Thomas was one of only three baritones to be included on that record. His aria was from Rossini's *Barber of Seville*: "Largo al Factotum." R.C.A. Victor also produced a record called Critics Choice, chosen by Irving Kolodin. On that record Thomas sang Massenet's "Salome! Salome!" from *Herodiade*.

During 1945-46 Thomas was the soloist each Sunday evening on the "Westinghouse Hour," a national radio hook-up from New York City. He sang ballads, opera numbers, and hymns to millions who dearly loved him. He became a household name and favorite. He ended each program with the tender words, "good night, mother." He also appeared frequently on other national radio programs such as "Five Star Theater," "R.C.A. Magic Key," "Ford Sunday Evening Hour," "The Pause that Refreshes on the Air," and the "Bell Telephone Hour."

I heard Mr. Thomas in person on six different occasions. He was the greatest baritone "vocalist" I ever heard, but not the greatest singing-actor. This accolade would have to go to Lawrence Tibbett. Like John McCormack, Thomas' world-wide fame came largely from outside the field of opera – from concerts, radio, and recordings. Mr. Thomas was the favorite male singer of Mrs. Blair and our daughters Kathleen and Barbara.

My readers may be interested in an amusing incident or two from Thomas' career. After he had sung without stint for more than two hours in a concert – he always gave his utmost, so as to never short-change his devoted audience – a man from the second balcony in Seattle called out, "Mr. Thomas, please sing the prologue from *Pagliacci*." Mr. Thomas, having already included in his program five great opera arias, apparently felt the request was a very unfair one. So he cupped his hands to his mouth and called back, "If you want to hear the Prologue, you can have the auditorium after I'm gone."

Among several sports by which Mr. Thomas kept "in shape" was golfing. When he retired to Apple Valley, California, he bought a home near a golf course so he could play every day. Very often in the clubhouse shower room, after rounds of golf, Mr. Thomas would begin singing. On one occasion he "let out" a great tone – perhaps an A flat – to which a fellow in the next stall roared out, "Who do you think you are, John Charles Thomas?"

A more endearing moment was after a Thomas concert in Seattle in 1937. With several hundred people greeting him on stage after the performance, he took one of Mrs. Blair's hands in his and held it while we chatted with him for several minutes.

Mrs. Blair and I often discussed why Mr. Thomas held her hand and seemed to give us extra time. We concluded that he saw our attire – Mrs. Blair was wearing a summer coat, in cold weather; she had no furs and jewels, and I was wearing an altered, "hand-me-down" suit. This was in the depression, and I was just getting started in my profession, and we had very little money. I am sure that Mr. Thomas compared us with the very well dressed, wealthy people, all around us, and said to himself, "this young couple must love music, very much, to come to the concert instead of putting the money on their backs." Although we recognized the beautiful, God-given voice of Mr. Thomas, this incident also caused us to see the big soul of this great man.

Many years later (in 1946) I wrote to Mr. Thomas. He answered my letter with a very warm "thank you" and friendly greeting.

# LAWRENCE TIBBETT

Lawrence Tibbett, baritone, was born in Bakersfield California, on November 16, 1896, and died in New York City on July 15, 1960. His youth was spent in Los Angeles, where he studied singing with Basil Ruysdael. In 1921 he appeared as a concert singer, and in 1923 he continued the study of voice with Frank La Forge in New York. That same year he made his Metropolitan debut in a small role in *Boris Godounov*. This led to an appearance there on January 2, 1925 in the role of Ford in *Falstaff*. He took the house by storm, and was accorded a long ovation, in a cast that was headed by Antonio Scotti. The audience loved Tibbett so much that the clamor was much greater for him than it was for the famous Scotti. From that time on Tibbett was on the road to operatic greatness.

Around 1930, when Mr. Tibbett was starting to get some major roles at the Met, his competition consisted of great baritones who were soon to leave the company – such stars as Scotti, Ruffo, De Luca, Danise, and Basiola.

Ruffo, with the huge voice, who many critics claimed was the greatest baritone of all time, was a great Barnaba, Scotti a fine Scarpia, De Luca a superb Rigoletto, Danise an outstanding Gerard, and Basiola a splendid Tonio. With Stracciari to boot, who some authorities thought had the most beautiful voice of all, Tibbett was in the midst of gigantic competition. However, he was equal to the circumstances, and even without the impending retirements of the singing giants just mentioned, because of his great range of abilities Tibbett would have had a great career at the Met whether or not his competition remained there.

Tibbett was a six footer, not portly, quite good looking, with a magnificent resonant speaking voice and an infectious laugh and smile. He was a consummate artist. He had the soft, beautiful tones which made his big ones, by contrast, all the more thrilling. His breath control, and "way with a song" or aria were remarkable in artistry. I heard him many times. He became one of my absolute favorites.

After 1934, when Thomas joined the Met, Tibbett's most serious competition until he retired was: Thomas, Bonelli, Warren, and Merrill.

Lawrence Tibbett as Figaro
in *The Barber of Seville*

A fine music critic of the period, the still active Henry Pleasants, was a Tibbett and Thomas admirer. I wrote to Mr. Pleasants and asked him how he compared the two as singers. Mr. Pleasants wrote back and said among other things, "Mr. Thomas was the greater vocalist, and Mr. Tibbett was the greater man of the theater." I presume that Mr. Pleasants meant that Mr. Tibbett was the greater actor.

Mr. Tibbett sang in 1937 at Covent Garden as Scarpia in *Tosca*. His concerts took him to all the international music centers. He sang as far away as New Zealand and Australia. Although his greatest roles were as an interpreter of Verdi and Puccini, he also sang in world premiers of *The King's Henchman, Peter Ibbetson, The Emperor Jones, and Merry Mount*.

At the height of his career, his concerts would be sold out for weeks in advance. The managements would put chairs on the stage, behind Mr. Tibbett, in order to seat some of the overflow crowds.

Besides his twenty-five years in opera-and-concert singing and the making of many recordings, he performed in at least five motion pictures for Metro-Goldwyn-Mayer. His popularity was enormous.

Among baritones, I believe that in his prime Mr. Tibbett was surely one of the greatest singing-actors of all time. Tito Gobbi was an exceptional singing-actor, with emphasis on actor. But his voice did not have the beauty of a Tibbett, Thomas, Warren, Merrill, or Bastianini.

A baritone in Mr. Tibbett's era who should not be forgotten is Nelson Eddy. While Mr. Eddy sang in opera early in his career, most of his renown came from his many Hollywood motion pictures, his concerts and his recordings. In his last years he had a steady series of night club appearances.

Mr. Eddy had a big, attractive voice, but he in no way measured up to Tibbett's opera career, or to Mr. Tibbett's fame as a world-class singer.

98

Leonard Warren as Iago
in *Otello*

# LEONARD WARREN

Leonard Warren, baritone, was born April 21, 1911, in New York, and died March 4, 1960. He attended Columbia University. After singing in the chorus of the Radio City Music Hall in 1935, he studied with Sidney Dietch in New York and with Giuseppe Païs and Riccardo Picozzi in Milan, Italy. In 1939 he made his debut at the Metropolitan as Paolo Albani in *Simone Boccanegra*. Mr. Warren was especially admired in the baritone roles from the Italian operatic literature. He made highly successful guest appearances in San Francisco, Chicago, Mexico City, the Teatro Colón, and the Rio de Janeiro Opera. He was honored further by being given the opportunity to sing the lead baritone roles in *Otello* and *Rigoletto*, at La Scala in 1953. In 1958 he toured Russia, singing in such places as Moscow and Kiev.

In 1960 Mr. Warren died suddenly on the stage at the Metropolitan in a performance of *La Forza del Destino*. His death was a tremendous loss to the opera world.

I had the privilege of hearing Leonard Warren in Palo Alto, California, the evening of April 23, 1951, on the campus of Stanford University. My wife, Marguerite, daughters Kathleen and Barbara, and I had one of the great treats of our lives in hearing Mr. Warren when he was at the height of his vocal powers. He started out slowly, as most singers do in getting warmed up, and then he proceeded to almost literally take the "house down." The applause with "bravos" was tremendous. Among other great arias he sang the "Credo" from *Otello*, the "Avant de quitter" from *Faust*, the "Largo Al Factotum" from the *Barber of Seville*, and the "Prologue" from *Pagliacci*. Willard Sektberg was at the piano.

With the vocal decline of Lawrence Tibbett in the early 1940s and John Charles Thomas devoting more and more time to concert and radio work, Leonard Warren became the number one baritone at the Metropolitan. He worked very hard and painstakingly to improve his tone production, which was always excellent, and to increase the number of roles that he could perform. There is no doubt in my mind that from about 1947 to 1960, the year of his death, Warren was the greatest baritone in the world. He had a rich, seamless voice from top to bottom, with almost unlimited power and range.  Some of the baritones at the Met with whom he shared roles were:  Merrill, Bastianini, MacNeil, Guarrera, Gobbi, Valdengo, Sereni, Capecchi, London, and Weede.

Other baritones of the Warren era, singing very well elsewhere, were: Bechi, Gorin, Protti, Glossop, Taddei, Guelfi, Krause, Fischer-Dieskau, Bacquier, Evans and Panerai.  Some of these were to sing at the Metropolitan later on.

Immediately following Mr. Warren's death, Anselmo Colzani, with a powerful and sonorous voice, took over a number of Warren's roles.  But it was Robert Merrill who became Mr. Warren's successor as the greatest baritone in the world.

# ROBERT WEEDE

Robert Weede, baritone, was born in 1903, in Baltimore, Maryland. He began his opera career in 1927 with the De Feo Opera Company. After winning the Caruso Memorial Prize, he went to Milan and studied with Oscar Anselmi. He made guest appearances on a number of stages in the United States before he was engaged in 1933 by Roxy Rothafel to sing at the Radio City Music Hall in New York City.

Mr. Weede sang at the Metropolitan Opera from 1936-42 and then again from 1944-45, making his debut as Tonio in *I Pagliacci*. Because of his outstanding voice, many people have wondered why the Metropolitan did not use Mr. Weede more than it did. However, the San Francisco Opera Company was glad for that neglect and engaged Mr. Weede regularly for over a period of twenty years.

Mr. Weede was also a hit on Broadway. He starred in such musicals as *Milk and Honey* and the *Most Happy Fellow*.

On September 8, 1947, Weede sang the role of Amonasro in *Aïda* at the Civic Auditorium in Seattle. It was with the San Francisco Opera Company. The conductor was Paul Breisach. Weede's Amonasro was acclaimed by the press as outstanding. His colleagues were Roman, Thebom, Baum, Moscona, Alvary, and Votipka.

I heard Mr. Weede again at the Orpheum Theater in Seattle as *Rigoletto* on May 6, 1954. His "Pari siamo" and "Cortigiani vil razza dannata" were superbly done. In the cast with him were John Crain and Graciela Rivera. The conductor was Eugene Linden.

I believe that Robert Weede was a very superior baritone. Except his acclaim on Broadway and in cities such as San Francisco, Seattle, and a number of others, he did not receive the recognition he deserved.

# BASSES

Salvatore Baccaloni
in *Gianni Schicchi*

# SALVATORE BACCALONI

Salvatore Baccaloni, bass, was born April 14, 1900, in Rome. As a child he sang in the Sistine Chapel Choir. He later thought he would like to become an architect. During those studies he used his free time to study voice with Giuseppe Kaschmann. In 1922 he made his debut at the Teatro Adriano as Bartolo in *Ill Barbiere di Siviglia*.

Mr. Baccaloni then sang with considerable success at La Scala and on the other large Italian stages. After 1930 he appeared frequently in South America, particularly at the Teatro Colón. He was also a frequent and very welcome guest at Covent Garden. He sang in the world premieres of many operas: in Rome, 1933, also in Rome, 1935; Venice, 1938; and from 1936 to 1939 he was much admired both at the Glyndebourne and Salzburg Festivals, particularly for his portrayal of Bartolo in the *Ill Barbiere di Siviglia*.

From 1940-47, Baccaloni had great triumphs at the Metropolitan Opera. He was also very much admired in San Francisco. In his last years of singing he was famous in comic film roles.

I heard Mr. Baccaloni in Seattle in 1946 with Kirsten and Kullman in *La Bohème* in the San Francisco Opera Company's production. Again in 1960 Baccaloni appeared in *Tosca* with the San Francisco Opera Company at the War Memorial Opera House. Some of his partners for the evening were Zampieri, Kirsten, Gobbi, and Foldi. I again enjoyed Mr. Baccaloni in this role of Sacristan.

In my opinion Mr. Baccaloni was the best basso-buffo of his generation. He had a big voice and was an outstanding actor. In the title role of *Falstaff* he has scarcely been excelled.

Another great basso-buffo in our time was Fernando Corena.

Jerome Hines as Sarastro
in *Die Zauberflöte*

# JEROME HINES

Jerome Hines, bass, was born in Hollywood, California in 1921. He first studied chemistry and mathematics at the University of California at Los Angeles. After his work there he studied voice with Gennaro Cuni and made his debut at the San Francisco Opera Company in *Tannhäuser* in the season of 1940-41. His role was that of Biterolf.

Mr. Hines sang opera in New Orleans and performed with a number of American orchestras. The Metropolitan Opera Company gave him a contract in 1946. He remained there for many years and broke Antonio Scotti's record for longevity at that revered opera company.

Guest appearances brought Mr. Hines great success at the opera houses in Rio de Janeiro, São Paulo, Mexico City, and the Teatro Colón. In 1953 he sang Nick Shadow in *The Rake's Progress* at the Edinburgh Festival. In 1954 he was given great acclaim in Munich for his role of Don Giovanni. He later made brilliant guest appearances at the Paris Opéra, the Vienna State Opera, The Rome Opera, the Maggio Musicale Festival, and in 1959 at La Scala. He appeared a number of times after 1958 at the Bayreuth Festivals.

I heard Mr. Hines at the War Memorial Opera House in San Francisco during the 1940-41 season. He was in a cast that could hardly be excelled. The other members were Pons, Peerce, and Tibbett in the opera *Rigoletto* The crowd reaction was virtual pandemonium. Mr. Hines is also a composer of music. His autobiography *This is My Story, This is My Song* was published in 1968.

I last heard Mr. Hines at the Seattle Opera House in 1986. He had written a religious play entitled *I am the Way*. He had the leading role, that of Christ. His tremendous voice was nothing short of magnificent and his acting seemed inspired. The staging was beautiful and the orchestration outstanding. The audience gave him and the entire cast a tremendous ovation at the conclusion of the oratorio. The production was sponsored by Seattle Pacific University.

Mr. Hines should certainly be placed among the top half dozen great basses of our century. He is in the company of Chaliapin, Mardones, Pinza, Kipnis, and Siepi. Hines, an American, in my opinion is the best bass this country has produced.

# ALEXANDER KIPNIS

Alexander Kipnis, bass, was born on February 1, 1891, in Shitomire, Russia. At first he planned to go into business, but he soon decided to study singing at the conservatories in Warsaw and Berlin. In World War I he was interned in Berlin because he was a Russian. Later freed, he made his opera debut in 1916 at the Hamburg Opera.

Mr. Kipnis sang at Weisbaden from 1916-19 and at the German Opera House in Berlin-Charlottenburg from 1919-30. He traveled through the United States with the German Opera Company in 1929. He sang very often at the Chicago Opera from 1924-32. During those years he appeared frequently at La Scala, the Paris Opera, the Teatro-ColÂn, and the opera houses in Vienna and Munich. He was the number one bass at the Berlin State Opera from 1932-35.

Mr. Kipnis was admired at Salzburg and had many triumphs in England, North and South America, Australia, and New Zealand. He made his debut at the Metropolitan Opera in 1940 as Gurnemanz in *Parsifal*. He remained a principal bass in that great company until 1952. He also appeared with outstanding success at the San Francisco Opera.

I heard Mr. Kipnis in San Francisco in the opera *Tristan and Isolde* in 1939, with Flagstad, Meisle, and Melchior in the cast. A better cast for this opera than Flagstad, Melchior and Kipnis can hardly be imagined.

Mr. Kipnis had a large and beautifully developed bass voice. His equals could only be singers such as Chaliapin, Pinza, Siepi, Hines, and the present day great Nicolai Ghiaurov.

## EZIO PINZA

Ezio Pinza, bass, was born May 18, 1892, in Rome, and died May 9, 1957 in Stamford, Conn.   Early in his years he wanted to become a professional bicycle rider but gave up that idea and studied singing at the conservatories in Ravenna and Bologna with Ruzza and Vizzani.   He made his opera debut in Spezia in 1914 as Oroveso in *Norma*.

Mr. Pinza served in the Italian army in World War I.   After that service he took up his singing career again in 1919 at the Teatro Verdi in Florence.   In 1921 he went to La Scala, where he was highly successful. There he sang in several world premiéres, such as *Debora e Jaele* in 1922 and in Boito's *Nerone* in 1924.   Arturo Toscanini loved Pinza's voice and saw to it that he was assigned important roles at La Scala.

In 1926 Mr. Pinza was engaged by the Metropolitan Opera to make his debut as the High Priest in Spontini's *La Vestale*.   Until 1948 he was the principal bass in the Italian wing at the Metropolitan.   Mr. Pinza was highly successful in guest appearances at Covent Garden, the Paris Opéra, the Vienna State Opera, the Arena and Maggio Musicale Festivals, and on other important stages.   At the Salzburg Festivals he was acclaimed for his singing in memorable productions of *Don Giovanni* and *Le Nozze di Figaro* under the direction of Arturo Toscanini.   He also sang in Hollywood films.   After 1948, when he had given up his operatic career, he appeared in musicals and operettas, such as *South Pacific*, and in concerts.

In the 1938-39 season I heard Ezio Pinza in San Francisco in one of his greatest roles, that of *Don Giovanni*.   He absolutely took the house by storm in one of the few operas in which the bass has the title role.   He had a superb cast to augment his great singing – Rethberg, Jessner, Favero, Baccaloni, and Borgioli.   The conductor was Fritz Reiner.   I also heard Pinza in Seattle in 1946, when the San Francisco Opera company was touring there. His partners at that time were Dorothy Kirsten and Charles Kullman.   The opera was *La Bohéme*.

Mr. Pinza had a big, warm-timbred, flexible voice.   He sang over seventy operatic roles and was an actor of tremendous ability.   I firmly

Ezio Pinza
in *Don Giovanni*

believe that he and Chaliapin were the two best basses of our century with Siepi close behind.    Other outstanding basses I should mention are Mardones, Journet, Kipnis, Baccaloni, Christoff, Hines, Tozzi, Corena, and Rossi-Lemeni.

More recent basses who are regarded very highly are:   Raimondi, Ghiaurov, Talvella, Ghiusalev, Díaz, Moll, Treigle, Plishka, Howell, Lloyd, and Giaiotti.

Paul Plishka as Ramfis
in *Aïda*

# PAUL PLISHKA

Paul Plishka, bass, was born August 28, 1941, in Old Forge, Pa. He studied voice with Armen Boyajian, and made his debut in opera as Colline in *La Bohéme* with the Metropolitan Opera National Company in 1966.

Mr. Plishka sang opera in Canada – in Ottawa, and Vancouver. In Italy he sang at the Spoleto Festival and at La Scala. In the United States he has appeared in opera in the following cities: Hartford, Newark, New Orleans, New York (Met), Philadelphia (Lyric Opera), and in Pittsburgh, to name a few.

Some of the composers of major operas in which Mr. Plishka has participated are: Bellini, Mozart, Puccini, Verdi, and Wagner.

In 1986 I heard Mr. Plishka sing in Vancouver, Canada, during the World Festival, with the La Scala Grand Opera Company. On that occasion the opera was Verdi's *I Lombardi*, with Maestro Gavazzeni conducting.

It was a wonderful production. The staging, including the lighting, was indeed impressive. The La Scala chorus of 116 members plus 103 members in the La Scala orchestra, with the famous soloists, made for one of the greatest total opera productions I have ever witnessed.

Mr. Plishka has a big, beautiful, bass voice, and his acting was superb. He is one of the top bass voices in his category in the world today. I was also very pleased with the singing of Elizabeth Connell and that of Veriano Luchetti.

Among basses actively singing today Mr. Plishka shares the quality of singing produced by Ghiaurov, Raimondi, Ghiuselev, and Talvela.

Georgio Tozzi as Plunkett
in *Martha*

# GEORGIO TOZZI

Georgio Tozzi, bass, was born on January 8, 1923, in Chicago, of Italian extraction. He started out as a concert singer, but after studying in Italy and a guest appearance at La Scala, he was offered a contract to sing at the Metropolitan Opera in 1955.

Mr. Tozzi had great success at the Met as Figaro in *Le Nozze di Figaro*, as Don Basilio in *Il Barbiere di Siviglia*, and as Arkel in *Pelléas et Melisande*. In 1958 he sang the part of the Doctor in the world première of *Vanessa* at the Met.

Mr. Tozzi has also sung at the Salzburg Festival, in Chicago, in San Francisco, at the Vienna State Opera, and at the several leading Italian opera houses. He has also sung in such musicals as *South Pacific* and *The Student Prince*.

I heard Mr. Tozzi at the San Francisco Opera House in 1959-60 as Ramfis in *Aïda*. Other cast members were Price, Dalis, Vickers, and Weede. The conductor was Molinari-Pradelli.

Mr. Tozzi has a very flexible, large, and expressive bass voice. Although he sings all the bass roles, his range is such that he can very well be called a bass-baritone.

Some of Mr. Tozzi's competitors for the bass roles have been: Siepi, Corena, Vinco, Alvary, Tajo, Moscona, Modesti, Baccaloni, and Hines.

# ACTIVE
# PRESENT DAY
# SOPRANOS, TENORS, MEZZO-SOPRANOS,
# BARITONES AND BASSES

# ACTIVE, PRESENT DAY
# SOPRANOS, TENORS, MEZZO-SOPRANOS,
# BARITONES, AND BASSES

Because of the nationally televised opera productions, concerts, and other media exposure, I am not going to give you, my readers, an extended account of the lives of those singers in each voice category whom I believe to be among the greatest in the world today. You have heard them and read about them. I will give just a few facts about each.

## SOPRANOS

Montserrat Caballé, lyric soprano, Spanish, born, April 12, 1933, Barcelona, Spain. She is treated more fully elsewhere in this book.

Renata Scotto, lyric soprano, Italian, born, February 24, 1933, Savona, Italy. Greater attention given to her elsewhere in this book.

Mirella Freni, lyric soprano, Italian, born, February 27, 1935, Modena, Italy.

Teresa Stratas, lyric soprano, Canadian, born, May 26, 1938, Toronto, Canada. She is treated more fully elsewhere in this book.

Teresa Zylis-Gara, soprano, lirico-spinto, born, January 23, 1935, Wilno, Poland.

Katia Ricciarelli, lyric soprano, Italian, born in Rovigo, Italy.

Kiri Te Kanawa, lyric soprano, New Zealander, born in Gisborne, New Zealand.

Martina Arroyo, spinto, American, born in New York.

Other great sopranos whom we will also want to watch as their careers continue: Ileana Cotrubas, Ghena Dimitrova, Eva Marton, Margaret Price, Julia Varady, and Edita Gruberova. Carol Vaness, whom I just heard in Seattle (1987) as Desdemona, is well on her way to becoming one of the world's fine sopranos.

## TENORS

Luciano Pavarotti, lyric tenor, Italian, born, October 12, 1935, Modena, Italy.

Placido Domingo, tenor, Spanish, born, January 21, 1941, Madrid, Spain.

José Carreras, lyric tenor, Spanish, born in Barcelona, Spain. Greater attention given to him elsewhere in this book.

120

Alfredo Kraus, lyric tenor, Spanish, born, November 24, 1927, Las Palmas, Canary Islands, Spain.

John Vickers, heldentenor, Canadian, born October 29, 1926, Prince Albert, Sask.

Giacomo Aragall, lyric tenor, Spanish, born, June 6, 1939, Barcelona, Spain.

Stuart Burrows, lyric tenor, British, born, February 7, 1933, Pontypridd, Wales.

Giuseppe Giacomini, lyric spinto tenor, Italian, born, September 7, 1940, Padua, Italy.

Veriano Luchetti, lyric tenor, Italian, born, March 12, 1939, Tuscania,Italy.

Carlo Cossutta, dramatic tenor, Italian, born, May 8, 1932, Trieste, Italy.

James McCracken, dramatic tenor, American, born, December 16, 1926, Gary, Indiana.

James King, dramatic tenor, American, born, May 22, 1925, Dodge City, Kansas.

Renato Cioni, lyric tenor, Italian, born, April 15, 1929, Portoferraio, Italy.

## MEZZO-SOPRANOS

Agnes Baltsa, lyric coloratura mezzo-soprano, Greek, born November 19, 1944, Lefkas, Greece.

Grace Bumbry, dramatic mezzo-soprano, American, born St. Louis, Missouri.

Irene Dalis, dramatic mezzo-soprano, American, born October 8, 1930, San Jose, CA.

Teresa Berganza, coloratura mezzo-soprano, Spanish, born March 16, 1935, Madrid, Spain.

Fiorenza Cossotto, lyric and dramatic mezzo-soprano, Italian, born April 22, 1935, Crescentino/Vercelli, Italy.

Tatiana Troyanos, dramatic mezzo-soprano, American, born September 12, 1938, New York.

Brigitte Fassbaender, mezzo-soprano, German, born July 3, 1939, Berlin, Germany.

Huguette Tourangeau, contralto, Canadian, born August 12, 1938, Montreal, Canada.

Shirley Verrett, lyric and dramatic mezzo-soprano, American, born May 31, 1931, New Orleans, LA.

Frederica Von Stade, lyric mezzo-soprano, American, born Somerville, N. J.

Christa Ludwig, mezzo-soprano, German, born March 16, 1928, in Berlin, Germany.

Rita Gorr, mezzo-soprano, born February 18, 1926, Ghent, Belgium.

Marilyn Horne, mezzo-soprano, American, born January 16, 1934, Bradford, PA. Treated more fully elsewhere in this book.

Elena Obraztsova, mezzo-soprano, Russian, born July 7, 1939, Leningrad, Russia.

## BARITONES

Sherrill Milnes, dramatic baritone, American, born January 10, 1935, Downers Grove IL.

Dietrich Fischer-Dieskau, lyric baritone, German, born May 28, 1925, Berlin, Germany.

Piero Cappuccilli, dramatic baritone, Italian, born November 9, 1929, Trieste, Italy.

Renato Bruson, dramatic baritone, Italian, born January 13, 1936, Granze/Padera, Italy.

Matteo Manuguerra, lyric baritone, French, born October 5, 1924, Tunisia.

Vincenzo Sardinero, lyric baritone, Spanish, born January 12, 1937, Barcelona, Spain.

Louis Quilico, dramatic baritone, Canadian, born January 14, 1930, Montreal, Canada.

Ingvar Wixwell, lyric baritone, Swedish, born 1931 in Lulea, Sweden.

Hermann Prey, lyric baritone, German, born July 11, 1929, Berlin, Germany.

Eberhard Wächter, dramatic baritone, Austrian, born July 9, 1929, Vienna, Austria.

Kari Nurmela, dramatic baritone, Finnish, born May 26, 1937, Viipuri, Finland.

Yuri Mazurok, lyric baritone, Russian, born July 18, 1931, Krasnik, U.S.S.R.

Leo Nucci, lyric baritone, Italian, born 1942 near Bologna, Italy.

Pablo Elvíra, lyric baritone, American, born September 24, 1938 in Puerto Rico.

## BASSES

Bonaldo Giaiotti, bass, Italian, born December 25, 1932, Ziracco, Udine, Italy.

Nicolai Ghiaurov, bass, Bulgarian, born September 13, 1929, Velingrad, Bulgaria.

Nicola Ghiuselev, bass, Bulgarian, born August 17, 1936, Pavlikeni, Bulgaria.

Justino Díaz, bass, Puerto Rican, born January 29, 1940, San Juan, Puerto Rico.

Ezio Flagello, bass, American, born, January 28 1933, in New York.

Paul Plishka, bass, American, born August 29, 1941, Old Forge, PA. He is treated more fully elsewhere in this book.

Martti Talvela, bass, Finnish, born February 4, 1935, Hiitola, Finland.

Kurt Moll, bass, German, born April 11, 1938, Buir, Germany.

Ruggero Raimondi, bass-baritone, Italian, born October 3, 1944, Bologna, Italy.

Samuel Ramey, bass, American, born March 28, 1942, Colby, Kansas.

James Morris, bass-baritone, American, born, January 10, 1947, Baltimore, MD.

Robert Lloyd, bass, British, born, March 2, 1940, South-end-on-Sea, United Kingdom.

José Van Dam, bass-baritone, Belgian, born, August 25, 1940, Brussels, Belgium.

**OTHER SINGERS**
**PAST AND PRESENT**
**WHOM I REGARD HIGHLY**

## OTHER SINGERS, PAST AND PRESENT, WHOM I REGARD HIGHLY

Bessie Abott
Theo Adam
Frances Alda
John Alexander
Luigi Alva
Pasquale Amato
Elly Ameling
Mario Ancona
Peter Anders
Gabor Andrasy
Giuseppe Anselmi
Francisco Araiza
Angelo Bada
Janet Baker
John Baker
Georges Baklanoff
Rose Bampton
Sari Barabas
Daniele Barioni
Maria Barrientos
Mattia Battistini
Kathleen Battle
Erna Berger
Walter Berry
Richard Best
Siguard Bjoerling
Ingrid Bjoner
Ernest Blanc
Judith Blegen
Kurt Bohme
Michael Bohnen
Allesandro Bonci
Celestina Boninsegna
Franco Bonisolli
Armando Borgioli
Inge Borkh
Géori Boué
Vina Bovy
Karen Branzell
Sophie Braslau
Gre Brouwenstein
Lucielle Browning
Lina Bruna-Rasa
Sesto Bruscantini
Emma Calvé
Giuseppe Campanari
Giuseppe Campora
Maria Caniglia

Margherita Carosio
Rosanna Carteri
Mariano Caruso
Anna Case
Walter Cassel
Lina Cavalieri
Marie Cebotari
Anita Cerquetti
Mario Chamlee
Renato Cesari
Lili Chookasian
Gina Cigna
Marie Collier
Ferruccio Corradetti
Dominic Cossa
Franz Crass
Giulio Crimi
Richard Cross
Gilda Cruz-Romo
Diane Curry
Phyllis Curtin
Toti Dal Monte
Charles Dalmores
Ryland Davies
Emilio De Gogorza
Elvira De Hidalgo
John Del Carlo
Libero De Luca
Fernando De Lucia
Alessio De Paolis
Édouard De Reszke
Michel Dens
Anton Dermota
Emmy Destin
Christina Deutekom
Enrico Di Giuseppe
Nicholas Di Virgilio
Adamo Didur
Andreas Dippel
Mattiwilda Dobbs
Helen Donath
Dale Duesing
Mignon Dunn
Emma Eames
Florence Easton
Otto Edelman
Minnie Egener
Brent Ellis

Cloe Elmo
Mafalda Favero
Jean Fenn
Eugenio Fernandi
Kathleen Ferrier
Agostino Ferrin
Mario Filippeschi
Cesare Formichi
Dino Formichini
Maureen Forrester
Paul Franke
Olive Fremstad
Gottlob Frick
Johanna Gadski
Maria Galvany
Mary Garden
John Garris
Mabel Garrison
Maria Gay
Leyla Gencer
Dusolina Giannini
Joao Gibin
Dinh Gilly
Hertha Glaz
Alma Gluck
Donald Gramm
Louis Graveure
Reri Grist
Elizabeth Grümmer
Hilda Gueden
Joan Hammond
Shirley Harned
Mack Harrell
Hilda Harris
Clifford Harvuot
Elizabeth Harwood
Osi Hawkins
Roland Hayes
Thomas Hayward
Joshua Hecht
Frieda Hempel
Barbara Hendricks
Ludwig Hoffman
Hans Hopf
Hans Hotter
Giovanni Inghilleri
Maria Ivogun
Josephine Jacoby
Herbert Janssen
Helen Jepson
Raoul Jobin

Gwyneth Jones
Isola Jones
Edward Johnson
Julia Migenes Johnson
Sena Jurinac
Raina Kabaivanska
Linda Kelm
Robert Kerns
Diane Kesling
Margarete Klose
Sandor Kónya
Miliza Korjus
Erika Koth
Toni Kraemer
Jean Kraft
Heidi Krall
Fritz Krenn
Erich Kunz
Maria Kurenko
Maria Labia
Flaviano Labó
Forrest Lamont
Albert Lance
Bruno Landi
Marjorie Lawrence
Virgilio Lazzari
Evelyn Lear
Lilly Lehmann
Lotte Lehmann
Frida Leider
Brenda Lewis
Mary Lewis
Richard Lewis
William Lewis
Ilva Ligabue
Aroldo Lindi
Wilma Lipp
Martha Lipton
Emanuel List
Emmy Loose
Pilar Lorengar
Max Lorenz
John Macurdy
Jean Madeira
Philip Maero
René Maison
Catherine Malfitano
Dorothea Manski
Queena Mario
Lucy Isabelle Marsh
Lois Marshall

Riccardo Martin
Janis Martin
Enzo Mascherini
Edith Mason
Margarethe Matzenauer
Victor Maurel
Dorothy Maynor
Richard Mayo
Barry McDaniel
Nellie Melba
Luise Melchiorre
Carmen Melis
Francesco Merli
Mady Mesple
Joseph Metternich
Kerstin Meyer
Anne Michalsky
Janine Micheau
Mildred Miller
Leona Mitchell
Norman Mittelmann
José Mojica
Luigi Montesanto
Nicola Monti
Barry Morell
Maria Muller
Melitta Muszely
Michael Myers
Robert Nagy
Heddle Nash
Herva Nelli
Giulio Neri
Elena Nicolai
Elena Nikolaidi
Lillian Nordica
Jessye Norman
Jarmila Novotna
Margarethe Ober
Magda Oliviero
Fritz Ollendorf
Marie Olszewska
William Olvis
Sigrid Onegin
Lisa Otto
Iva Pacetti
Lina Pagliughi
Allessio Paolis
Kostas Paskalis
Julian Patrick
Adelina Patti
Peter Pears

Gino Penno
Flora Perini
Ivan Petrov
Marguerite Piazza
Alfred Piccaver
Pol Plancon
Rosalind Plowright
Hetti Plumacher
Afro Poli
Juan Pons
Carmela Ponselle
Lucia Popp
Giacinto Prandelli
Bruno Prevedi
Jaro Prohaska
Ruth-Margret Putz
Florence Quartararo
Gianni Raimondi
Rosa Raisa
Torsten Ralph
Judith Raskin
Eugenia Ratti
John Reardon
Paul Reimers
Maurice Renaud
Delia Rigal
Giacomo Rimini
Paul Robeson
Mado Robin
Margaret Roggero
Roger Roloff
Stella Roman
Helge Roswaenge
Léon Rothier
Michel Roux
Leonie Rysanek
Erna Sack
Mario Sammarco
Ada Sari
Sylvia Sass
Augusto Scampini
Heinrich Schlusnus
Joseph Schmidt
Rudolf Schock
Paul Schoffler
Peter Schreier
Elisabeth Schumann
Hanna Schwarz
Joseph Schwarz
Graziella Sciutti
Evelyn Scotney

Norman Scott
Jeanette Scovotti
Sara Scuderi
Bruno Sebastian
Andres Segurola
Marcella Sembrich
Neil Shicoff
George Shirley
Anja Silja
Paolo Silveri
Léopold Simoneau
Monica Sinclair
Martial Singher
Leo Slezak
Elisabeth Soderstrom
Enzo Sordello
Gerard Souzay
Erna Spoorenberg
Mariano Stabile
Sylvia Stahlmann
Hanny Steffek
Thomas Stewart
Teresa Stich-Randall
Rita Streich
Cheryl Studer
Elena Suliotis
Conchita Supervia
Set Svanholm
Alexander Sved
Jess Thomas
Hugh Thompson
Alan Titus
Anna Tomowa-Sintow
Theodor Uppman
Benita Valente
Frank Valentino
Richard Van Allan
Cyrena Van Gordon
Arnold Van Mill
Anton Van Rooy
Astrid Varnay
Josephine Veasey
Galina Vishnevskaya
David Ward
Sandra Warfield
Felicia Weathers
Ljuba Welitch
Andrew White
Wolfgang Windgassen
Fritz Wunderlich
Frances Yeend

Nicola Zaccaria
Guiseppe Zampieri
Mario Zanasi
Georgio Zancanaro
Virginia Zeani

# BIBLIOGRAPHY

# BIBLIOGRAPHY

Ardoin, John — *The Callas Legacy, a Biography of a Career.* Revised Edition, Charles Scribner's Sons, New York, 1977 and 1982.

Bing, Sir Rudolf — *A Knight at the Opera.* G. P. Putnam's Sons, New York, 1981.

Domingo, Placido — *My First Forty Years.* Alfred A. Knopf, New York, 1983.

Gobbi, Tito — *On His World of Italian Opera.* Franklin Watts, New York, 1984.

Harries, Meirion & Susie — *Opera Today.* St. Martin's Press, New York, 1986.

Horne, Marilyn with Jane Scovell — *Marilyn Horne, My Life*, Atheneum New York, 1983.

Kirsten, Dorothy — *A Time to Sing.* Doubleday & Co., Inc., Garden City, New York, 1982.

Kolodin, Irving — *The Opera Omnibus - Four Centuries of Critical Give and Take.* E. P. Dutton & Co., Inc. New York, 1982.

Kolodin, Irving — *The Metropolitan Opera - 1883-1966.* Alfred A. Knopf, New York. These are Borzoi Books.

Kutsch, K. J. and Riemens, Leo and Jones, Harry Earl — *A Concise Biographical Dictionary of Singers.* Chilton Book Company, Philadelphia, New York, London, 1962, 1966, and 1969.

Ledbetter, Gordon T. — *The Great Irish Tenor - John McCormack.* Charles Scribner's Sons, New York, 1977.

May, Robin — *A Companion to the Opera.* Lutterworth Press, Guildford and London, 1977.

132

| | |
|---|---|
| Mayer, Martin | *The Met - One Hundred Years of Grand Opera.* Simon & Schuster, New York, 1983, The Metropolitan Opera Guild, & Thames and Hudson, Ltd., London. |
| Pavarotti, Luciano with William Wright | *My Own Story.* Doubleday & Company, Inc., Garden City, New York, 1981. |
| Pleasants, Henry | *The Great Singers.* Simon and Schuster, New York, 1966. |
| Ponselle, Rosa Drake, James Forward by Luciano Pavarotti | *A Singer's Life.* A. Doubleday & Company, Inc., Garden City, New York, 1982. |
| Prawy, Marcel | *The Vienna Opera.* Praeger Publishers, New York, Washington 1970. |
| Rich, Maria F., Editor | *Who's Who In Opera.* Arno Press, A New York Times Company, New York, 1976. |
| Rosenthal, Harold | *Two Centuries of Opera at Covent Garden.* Putnam, - Great Russell Street, London, 1958. |
| Scotto, Renata and Octavia Roca | *Scotto More Than a Diva.* Doubleday & Company, Inc., Garden City, New York, 1984. |
| Sills, Beverly | *Bubbles - A Self Portrait by Beverly Sills.* Bobbs-Merrill, Indianapolis/ New York, 1976, Meridith Enterprises, Ltd. |
| Sutherland, Joan Brian Adams | *La Stupenda, A biography of Joan Sutherland.* Hutchinson of Australia, 1980. |
| Tucker, Richard | *A Biography.* James A. Drake, E. P. Dutton, Inc., New York, 1984. |
| Victor Talking Machine Company | *The Victor Book of the Opera.* R.C.A. Manufacturing Co., Inc., Camden, New Jersey U.S.A. 1929 and 1936. |

# INDEX

INDEX

Adler, Kurt Herbert: 21
Albanese, Licia: 3, 11, 15, 59, 79, 89
Althouse, Paul: 63
Alvary, Lorenzo: 101, 115
Amara, Lucine: 12
Amparan, Belen: 78
Anderson, Marian: 78
Anselmi, Oscar: 101
Aragall, Giacomo: 120
Arroyo, Martina: 12, 119
Baccaloni, Salvatore: 3, 23, 73, 105, 111, 115
Bacquier, Gabriel: 100
Baldassare-Tedeschi, Giuseppina: 3
Baltsa, Agnes: 78, 120
Bamboschek, Giuseppe: 53
Bang, Paul: 57
Barbieri, Fedora: 77, 78
Basiola, Mario: 95
Bastianini, Ettore: 27, 33,45, 63, 73, 75, 82, 83, 97, 100
Baum, Kurt: 101
Beattie, Herbert: 69
Bechi, Gino: 100
Beigel, Victor: 57
Bellini, Vincenzo: 5, 37, 113
Berganza, Teresa: 78, 120
Bergonzi, Carlo: 40, 45, 47, 65, 83, 89
Bernheimer, Martin: 6
Betarini, Rucciana: 82
Bing, Sir Rudolf: 40, 65, 82
Bjoerling, Jussi: 45, 47, 83, 89
Boito, Arrigo: 5
Bonynge, Richard: 31
Borgioli, Dino: 23, 109
Bori, Lucrezia: 93
Boyajian, Armen: 113
Bratt, Gillis: 7
Breisach, Paul: 101
Brownlee, John: 77
Bruson, Renato: 90, 121
Bumbry, Grace: 78
Burrows, Stuart: 120
Busch, Fritz: 71
Caball, Montserrat: 5, 33, 119

Callas, Maria: 12, 15, 23, 27, 33, 63, 83
Capecchi, Renato: 100
Cappuccilli, Piero: 90, 121
Carey, Clive: 31
Carreras, Jos: 27, 29, 37, 119
Caruso, Enrico: 9, 45, 53, 54, 55, 93
Casa, Lisa Della: 11
Castagna, Bruna: 77, 78
Cehanovsky, George: 3, 23, 79
Chaliapin, Feodor: 107, 108
Chapman, Frank: 91
Christoff, Boris: 111
Cilea, Francesco: 5
Cioni, Renato: 87, 120
Colzani, Anselmo: 100
Conley, Eugene: 51
Connell, Elizabeth: 113
Conner, Nadine: 77
Corelli, Franco: 15, 21, 39, 40, 45, 47, 65, 83, 89
Corena, Fernando: 83, 111, 115
Cossotto, Fiorenza: 78, 83, 120
Cossutta, Carlo: 120
Costa, Mary: 11, 71, 87
Cotogni, Antonio: 47
Cotrubas, Ileana: 5, 119
Craig, John: 85
Crain, John: 101
Crespin, Rgine: 15
Crooks, Richard: 41, 43, 55, 62
Culp-Dornay, Betsy: 11
Cuni, Gennaro: 107
D'Angelo, Gianna: 39
Dalis, Irene: 77, 78, 115, 120
Damrosch, Walter: 41
Dandridge, Dorothy: 69
Danise, Giuseppe: 71, 95
De Los Angeles, Victoria: 11
De Luca, Giuseppe: 93, 95
De Reszke, Jean: 91
Debussy, Claude: 17
Del Monaco, Mario: 40, 45, 47, 65, 83
Di Stefano, Giuseppe: 40, 45, 47, 65, 83
DÀaz, Justino: 111, 121
Dickens, Aida: 31

Dickens, John: 31
Dietch, Sidney: 99
Dimitrova, Ghena: 6, 119
Domingo, Placido: 37, 40, 47, 119
Dominguez, Oralia: 78
Donizetti, Gaetano: 5, 37
Dornay, Louis: 11
Eddy, Nelson: 97
Eggerth, Marta: 49
Elias, Roasalind: 77
Elmo, Cloe: 78
ElvÀra, Pablo: 90, 121
Enchaniz, Jos: 61
Evans, Geraint: 100
Farrar, Geraldine: 23
Farrell, Eileen: 12
Fassbaender, Brigitte: 120
Favero, Mafalda: 23, 109
Fermin, Adelin: 91
Fischer-Dieskau, Dietrich: 90, 100, 121
Flagello, Ezio: 121
Flagstad, Kirsten: 7, 15, 57, 108
Fleta, Miguel: 47
Flotow, Friedrich Von: 49
Foldi, Andrew: 105
Forsell, John: 36
Fredricks, Richard: 69
Freni, Mirella: 5, 6, 119
Friml, Rudolf: 91
Galli-Curci, Amelita: 18, 19, 25, 31, 91, 93
Gatti-Casazza, Giulio: 48
Gavazzeni, Gianandrea: 113
Gedda, Micolai: 45, 65
Gerunda, Alceste: 61
Ghiaurov, Nicolai: 108, 111, 113, 121
Ghiusalev, Nicola: 111, 113, 121
Giacomini, Giuseppe: 120
Giaiotti, Bonaldo: 111, 121
Gigli, Beniamino: 3, 47, 48, 53, 63, 93
Gilbert, William: 91
Giordano, Umberto: 5
Glossop, Peter: 100
Gobbi, Tito: 97, 100, 105
Gorin, Igor: 84, 85, 100
Gorostiaga, Albert di: 19

Gorr, Rita: 78, 120
Gounod, Charles: 5
Graf, Herbert: 77
Grenzebach, Ernst: 57
Gruberova, Edita: 119
Guarrera, Frank: 73, 100
Guelfi, Giangiacomo: 100
Gutheil-Schoder, Marie: 77
Hackett, Charles: 50
Harshaw, Margaret: 12
Hecht, Joshua: 71, 73
Herbert, Victor: 91
Herman, William: 17
Herold, Vilhelm: 57
Hines, Jerome: 107, 111, 115
Homer, Louise: 72, 78
Horne, Marilyn: 5, 45, 69, 78, 121
Howell, Gwynne: 111
Jacobsen, Schytte-Ellen: 7
Jeritza, Maria: 15, 23
Jessner, Irene: 23, 109
Jobin, Raoul: 79
Journet, Marcel: 111
Kanawa, Kiri te: 5, 6, 119
Kaschmann, Giuseppe: 105
Kiepura, Jan: 49
Kimball, Florence Page: 21
King, James: 40, 120
Kipnis, Alexander: 7, 57, 107, 108, 111
Kirsten, Dorothy: 3, 11, 50, 105, 109
Koch, Rita: 75
Kolodin, Irving: 89, 91, 93
KÂnya, S ndor: 21
Kostelanetz, Andre: 19
Kraus, Alfredo: 40, 45, 65, 83, 120
Krause, Tom: 90, 100
Kritz, Kari: 69
Kullman, Charles: 3, 11, 50, 105, 109
La Forge, Frank: 41, 95
Lanza, Mario: 65
Lauri-Volpi, Giacomo: 47
Lehar, Franz: 91
Leinsdorf, Erich: 77, 79
Leliva, Tadeusz: 49
Leoncavallo, Ruggiero: 5
Liebling, Estelle: 25

Linden, Eugene: 101
Lloyd, Robert: 111, 122
London, George: 100
Lucatello, Ettore: 73
Luchetti, Veriano: 113, 120
Ludwig, Christa: 77, 78, 120
MacDonald, Jeanette: 12
MacNeil, Cornell: 87, 100
Macurdy, John: 69
Mahler, Gustav: 72
Manton, Raymond: 69
Manuguerra, Matteo: 90, 121
Mardones, Jos: 107, 111
Marshall, Charles: 91
Martell, Richard: 71
Martinelli, Giovanni: 45, 47,
    53, 63
Marton, Eva: 119
Massenet, Jules: 5
Mazurok, Yuri: 121
McArthur, Edwin: 57
McCormack, John: 43, 47, 54,
    55, 62, 93
McCracken, James: 40, 45, 65,
    73, 120
Meisle, Kathryn: 57, 108
Melchior, Lauritz: 7, 45, 47,
    57, 108
Melton, James: 51
Merola, Gaetano: 3, 78
Merrill, Robert: 65, 89, 90, 97,
    100
Milanov, Zinka: 15, 21, 23, 33
Mildenburg, Anna Bahr: 57
Milnes, Sherrill: 90, 121
Modesti, Giuseppe: 115
Moffo, Anna: 11
Molinari-Pradelli, Francesco:
    21, 63, 73, 115
Moll, Kurt: 111, 122
Moore, Grace: 11
Morris, James: 27, 37, 122
Moscona, Nicola: 101, 115
Mozart, Wolfgang Amadeus: 5,
    113
Munsel, Patrice: 12
Muzio, Claudia: 13, 33
Nilsson, Birgit: 15, 21
Nucci, Leo: 90, 121
Nurmela, Kari: 121
O'Brien, Vincent: 54

Obratsova, Elena: 78, 121
Pas, Giuseppe: 99
Palumbo, Guido: 73
Panerai, Rolando: 90, 100
Patan, Franco: 85
Pavarotti, Luciano: 37, 40, 47,
    119
Pederzini, Gianna: 78
Peerce, Jan: 3, 45, 59, 65, 89,
    107
Pertile, Aureliano: 47
Peters, Roberta: 17, 18, 25, 31,
    60
Piccoli, Emilio: 61
Picozzi, Riccardo: 99
Pinza, Ezio: 3, 23, 77, 93, 107,
    108, 109
Pirazzini, Miriam: 78
Pleasants, Henry: 97
Plishka, Paul: 113, 122
Poggi, Gianni: 83
Pons, Lily: 3, 18, 19, 25,
    31, 107
Ponselle, Rosa: 15, 21, 23, 33,
    91, 93
Prtre, Georges: 71
Prey, Hermann: 121
Price, Leontyne: 15, 23, 33, 89,
    115
Price, Margaret: 119
Price, Walter: 82
Protti, Aldo: 100
Puccini, Giacomo: 5, 37, 97, 113
Quilico, Louis: 90, 121
Raimondi, Ruggero: 111, 113 122
Ramey, Samuel: 122
Reiner, Fritz: 23, 109
Resnik, Regina: 21, 71, 77, 78,
    79
Rethberg, Elizabeth: 15, 21, 33,
    77, 109
Ricciarelli, Katia: 5, 119
Rich, Alan: 39
Rivera, Graciela: 101
Roche, Agostino: 78
Roman, Stella: 101
Romberg, Sigmund: 91
Roosevelt, Franklin Delano: 89
Rosati, Enrico: 47
Rossi-Lemeni, Nicola: 73, 111
Rossini, Gioacchino: 5

Rothafel, Roxy: 101
Rothenberger, Anneliese: 11
Ruffo, Titta: 82, 95
Ruysdael, Basil: 95
Rysanek, Leonie: 11
Sabatini, Vincenzo: 54
Sardinero, Vincenzo: 121
Sayo, BidÈ: 25, 31, 77
Schipa, Tito: 13, 43, 47, 55, 61, 62, 91, 93
Schneider, Edwin: 55
Schorr, Friedrich: 87
Schumann-Heink, Ernestine: 72, 78
Schwarzkopf, Elizabeth: 12
Scotti, Antonio: 95, 107
Scotto, Renata: 5, 6, 15, 27, 29, 37, 83, 119
Sektberg, Willard: 99
Serafin, Tullio: 45, 73
Sereni, Mario: 100
Siepi, Cesare: 83, 107, 108, 111, 115
Sills, Beverly: 25, 31, 85
Simionato, Giulietta: 73, 75, 77, 78, 82
Steber, Eleanor: 12
Stella, Antonietta: 83
Stevens, Ris: 77, 78, 79
Stignani, Ebe: 78
Stracciari, Riccardo: 95
Stratas, Teresa: 5, 27, 29, 37, 119
Strauss, Johann,: 5
Sullivan, Arthur: 91
Sullivan, Brian: 51
Sutherland, Joan: 25, 31, 69, 89
Swarthout, Gladys: 77, 78, 79, 91
Taddei, Giuseppe: 100
Tagliabue, Carlo: 78
Tagliavini, Ferruccio: 62, 65
Tajo, Italo: 115
Talvella, Martti: 111, 113, 122
Tauber, Richard: 47, 55, 62
Tebaldi, Renata: 3, 15, 21, 23, 33, 63, 83, 89
Tetrazzini, Luisa: 19, 25, 31
Thebom, Blanche: 78, 101

Thomas, John Charles: 3, 13, 54, 91, 93, 94, 95, 97, 99
Thorborg, Kerstin: 77
Tibbett, Lawrence: 3, 41, 53, 93, 95, 107
Toscanini, Arturo: 23, 33, 47, 59, 63, 78, 89, 109
Tourangeau, Huguette: 78, 120
Tozzi, Georgio: 12, 111, 115
Traubel, Helen: 15
Treigle, Norman: 111
Troyanos, Tatiana: 78, 120
Tucci, Gabriella: 11
Tucker, Richard: 33, 40, 45, 47, 63, 65, 89
Tucker, Sara: 63
Valdengo, Giuseppe: 100
Valentino, Frank: 3
Valletti, Cesare: 62, 65, 73
Van Dam, Jos: 122
Vaness, Carol: 6, 119
Varady, Julia: 119
Varviso, Silvio: 87
Vennard, William: 69
Verdi, Giuseppe: 5, 37, 97, 113
Verna-Curtis, Mary: 12
Verrett, Shirley: 78, 120
Vickers, Jon: 40, 45, 65, 115, 120
Vinay, Ramon: 45
Vinco, Ivo: 83, 115
Von Leclair, Mariette: 72
Von Stade, Frederica: 78, 120
Votipka, Thelma: 3, 78, 101
Wchter, Eberhard: 121
Wagner, Richard: 5, 7, 15, 57, 113
Warfield, William: 21
Warren, Leonard: 3, 95, 99, 100
Watrin, Otto: 23
Weede, Robert: 79, 100, 101, 115
Westwang, Albert: 7
Wixell, Ingvar: 90, 121
Zamboni, Rainaldo: 48
Zampieri, Giuseppe: 105
Zenatello, Giovanni: 19
Ziliani, Alessandro: 78
Zylis-Gara, Teresa: 119